Ibsen's Heroines

Austrian / German Culture Series

- ☐ R. M. RILKE, *Poems 1912–1926*
- ☐ GOETHE, *Roman Elegies*
- ☐ LOU SALOMÉ, *Rilke*
- ☐ LOU SALOMÉ, *Nietzsche*
- ☐ LOU SALOMÉ, *Freud*
- ☐ LOU SALOMÉ, *Ibsen's Heroines*
- ☐ R. M. RILKE, *Worpswede Journal*
- ☐ M. HAMBURGER, *Variations*
- ☐ KARL KERÉNYI, *Excursions of a Hellenist*
- ☐ NIETZSCHE, *Dithyrambs of Dionysus*

Lou Salomé

IBSEN'S HEROINES

*edited, translated
and with an introduction by*
Siegfried Mandel

BLACK SWAN BOOKS

Acknowledgement is made to the following: Princeton University Press, for permission to quote from Rudolph Binion, *Frau Lou: Nietzsche's Wayward Disciple* (Copyright © 1968 by Princeton University Press); Barthold Fles Literary Agency, for permission to quote from H. F. Peters, *My Sister, My Spouse: A Biography of Lou Andreas-Salomé* (New York: W. W. Norton, 1962); Limes Verlag and Sigmund Freud Copyrights Ltd., for permission to quote from Georg Groddeck, *Der Mensch und sein Es*, ed. Margaretha Honegger (Wiesbaden, 1970).

First edition

Published by

BLACK SWAN BOOKS Ltd.
P. O. Box 327
Redding Ridge, CT 06876
ISBN 0-933806-28-0

Contents

For Elise, Joe, Sarah, and David

Acknowledgments

The long road toward the first publication in English of Lou Andreas-Salomé's collected interpretations of Ibsen's dramatic heroines (first published in book form as *Henrik Ibsens Frauen-Gestalten* in Jena by Eugen Diederichs in 1892) was eased by colleagues, editors, and friends who gave encouragement in different ways: Kathy Price, Elizabeth L. Huberman, J. Mitchell Morse, Martha Kinney, Harvey Gross, and John Walsh. Dorothy Mandel graciously shared time with Lou Salomé. Leland H. Chambers, of the University of Denver, published an earlier version of Salomé's essay "Ellida: The Lady from the Sea" in the *Denver Quarterly* (Winter 1979), and a previous draft of a section of her essay on Hedda, entitled "Lou Andreas-Salomé: 'A Shot—and Nothingness,' " appeared in *Continental Drifter*, vol. I, no. 1 (1984), edited by Edward Dorn. Lillian F. Robinson chaired the national competition for the committee on translations for the Eugene M. Kayden Prizes in the Humanities. It was a pleasure to receive its generous translation and publications award. My thanks to all.

—S. M.

Ibsen's Heroines

I have not written roles for actors and actresses.
I have written to portray human beings.

—Ibsen

Introduction

I N 1981, some forty-four years after her death, Lou Salomé was reincarnated at the commission of the Bavarian State Opera as the heroine and title figure of an opera premiered in Munich (*Lou Salomé* by Giuseppe Sinopoli). Composer, conductor, and certified psychiatrist, Sinopoli presided over the ghostly scenario which featured her encounter with Nietzsche, while sequels with Rilke and Freud are in the wings. Her first surrogate appearance on stage, however, may well have occurred in 1891 as Ibsen's Hedda Gabler, through an odd set of circumstances. Lou's first attraction to a man of genius was Ibsen, but her interpretations of his heroines have only become familiar to German and Scandinavian audiences, in the absence of English translations of her Ibsen essays. These essays not only chart her thoughts about women's confined roles in society but they also do abundant justice to Ibsen's creations.

I

AFTER MEETING Fräulein Lou (Louise) von Salomé in 1882 in Rome, the lonely philosopher Friedrich Nietzsche was neither the first

---

Two informative biographical studies in English are cited in this Introduction by author: H. F. Peters, *My Sister, My Spouse: A Biography of Lou Andreas-Salomé* (New York: Norton, 1962), and Rudolph Binion, *Frau Lou: Nietzsche's Wayward Disciple* (New Jersey: Princeton University Press, 1968); indispensable as a memoir is Lou Andreas-Salomé, *Lebensrückblick: Grundrisse einiger Lebenserinnerungen*, ed. Ernst Pfeiffer (Frankfurt-am-Main: Insel Verlag, 1968). The influence of the theater director Otto Brahm, as well as the contemporaneous critical reception of Ibsen's dramas, may be reconstructed through articles in *Ibsen auf der deutschen Bühne*, ed. Wilhelm von Friese (Tübingen: Niemeyer, 1976), and *Otto Brahm, Kritiken und Essays*, ed. Fritz Martini (Zürich, Artemis, [1964]).

nor certainly the last person to call the strikingly handsome Russian girl of twenty-one years the most gifted, the most reflective, and "the most intelligent of all women" he had ever the fortune or misfortune to encounter. With charm, intellect, literary sophistication, and strength of mind, she gained entry into European circles of the intelligentsia in all fields, who formed a veritable *Who's Who* of creative personages in the theater and publishing, of the written and the visual arts, in psychology and philosophy, and even in politics. Controlled, sublimated, spiritualized or crassly rampant at different times of her private life, her erotic drives inspired or distressed her male friends and lovers and caused two suicides. No wonder then that biographers and writers of memoirs have been fascinated by her life and have described her in roles varying from a modern version of the ancient *hetaira* to the subject of a psychiatric case history.

Shortly before her encounter with Nietzsche, Lou had clarified for herself the emancipated track she wished to pursue from the time she abandoned her home-nest in the Russian metropolis of St. Petersburg (1880) until her death in 1937 in the German university town of Göttingen. Leaving home meant independence and a wresting loose from the loving constraints and limiting conventions—despite considerable personal freedoms—of her family, particularly her mother "who would dearly have called upon all her sons to help bring me back dead or alive." But, "as I was of an egotistic mind, I was spared totally any regret or homesickness." From Zurich, where she acquitted herself brilliantly as a university student in the liberal arts, she assertively wrote home to a confidant who was critical of her newly-won personal life:

I can neither base my life on models nor make of my life a model for anyone; instead, I will most certainly fashion my life in my own way, whatever may come of it. With that, I need not represent any principle but something even more wonderful—something that resides within oneself and is warm with resounding life, something that jubilates and that wants out. . . . One cannot be happier than I am because the fresh-holy-gay war that is about to begin does not frighten me; on the contrary, let it begin. We shall see whether or not the most common so-called "insuperable barriers" erected by the world will turn out to be harmless chalk circles!

She closed the letter with a plea not for advice but for his retention of the confidence that had grown between them "since the day when I became what I have become through you: Your girl."

The excerpt from the letter might hardly seem strange if it had not been addressed to a clergyman, Hendrik Gillot. In relation to him, she developed a scenario that was to repeat itself several times in her life, a scenario that sounds almost fictional. To start with, her father Gustav was a general in the Russian Army and a state official who came from a family of Baltic Germans of Huguenot extraction. He was also a devout person who petitioned the Czar for permission to help found a Lutheran church in St. Petersburg. Quite early his daughter lost faith in a personal God or one whose existence depended upon theological proof. Out of respect and love for the old, grey general, her father, she avoided an open break with the Church but postponed her confirmation. In the meantime, Hendrik Gillot and his family were invited to St. Petersburg where, as an ordained minister of the Dutch Reformed Church and with the sponsorship of the Dutch embassy, he became pastor of a "rival" and more cosmopolitan church. His pulpit personality and oratory were as impressive as his broad cultural background from which he drew his rational and philosophical sermons. When at the urgings of a relative, the general's daughter attended a Gillot service, she felt that "a live human being had come into my dreamworld." A letter expressing her wish to see him netted her an invitation to his pastoral study. From her recollections, the scene was sentimental; the emotionally high-strung seventeen-year-old in tears was greeted by a worldly pastor, fifteen years her senior, who embraced her with open arms. Several critical months of clandestine meetings verged on the brink of an Héloïse and Abélard situation, but it never came to that. She matured intellectually under his tutelage and she rapidly filled notebooks on readings he recommended from literature to metaphysics, the philosophy of religion, and a range of works in French and German.

The emotional and intellectual idyll was interrupted by her father's death—which came as a shock, all the more since the father-daughter relationship had been very affectionate. He was as loving and chivalric toward her as he was to his wife, giving her an indelible sense of pride and freedom under the wings of authority and a comforting intimacy that, however, was not without attending psychological problems for her; she often acted the vixen, taking pleasure in his approbations as well as his punishments. As for her tutoring sessions with Gillot, a sense of integrity prompted her to reveal them to her mother. During the subsequent confrontation, the pastor proved so persuasive, however, that he was permitted to continue his tutoring, a mistake that was to bring him anguish. While his arousal became earthy when his pupil sat on his lap, her spiritualized and daughter-like near-worship of him continued unabated. When suddenly he proposed marriage, intending to abandon his wife and two daughters, Louise told him that she was neither ready to marry nor to accept a defrocked God-figure.

Like other young Russians of her class, she decided on an escape route to Zurich where she would continue studies at the University. Her mother reluctantly agreed, but an obstacle remained. She had left the church, and the Czarist government would not grant a personal passport without a confirmation certificate. Gillot suggested that he perform the required confirmation service abroad in the church of a friend in a small Dutch village. Not only did she agree, but she prescribed what turned out to be a curious ceremony. Despite her unwillingness to marry Gillot, she "feared like death" the separation that would necessarily follow the confirmation. For the closing words of the ceremony that brazenly resembled a marriage, she chose to put God's words into Gillot's mouth: "Fear not, for I have redeemed you; I have called you by name, you are mine" (Isaiah, 43:1). The nervous bridegroom-god-priest stumbled over her unpronounceable first name, Ljola in Russian, and then called her Lou, a name she retained for herself from then on. Fortunately, as Lou noted in her memoir, her mother who accompanied her did not comprehend a word of the blasphemy carried out in Dutch. "I only half-understood the surprising turn taken by my youthful love story. . . . The loved man disappeared as suddenly from my adoration as did my love of God earlier." Later when she reviewed the symbolic significance of what had taken place, she rationalized that it was not a marriage, though she knelt before Gillot, because in a true marriage both partners kneel in unison and are united before a mutual ideal. That idea was to form a key element in her thinking. Only a few times in her life was she able to experience that ideal with a partner.

Lou's actions were not calculated to hurt another person but to satisfy a sense of self that avowed responsibility only to oneself. It may also be that the influence of a bright and charming maiden aunt, named Caro, took hold. Caro believed that it is quite natural for a female to follow deep unconscious needs and "to snuggle up to" an admired male mentally and physically (as Lou had to her father): that is necessary for a personal development in an atmosphere of protectedness and a sense of *freedom*. On the other hand, Caro explained to her niece, a woman's rationality of mind demands a standing alone with the strength called *independence*. The opposition between freedom and independence, unconscious needs and the rational mind, could be reconciled only through a mutual uplifting and acceptance—not by a bowing down of one to the other and not by a surrender or submission. Only if these conditions prevail can a capable and independent woman—after a decisive struggle—settle peacefully into her "destiny." It was Caro who had brought the young girl to the first, fateful pulpit appearance of Gillot, and in Lou's relationship with him the beliefs of Caro were tested. Beyond Gillot, these beliefs became living dogma for Lou.

Despite disapproval and chagrin at her apparent capriciousness, Lou's family allowed her to develop with freedom and continued the financial support of her "independent" life abroad. Nevertheless it was her fate not to be able to find a man for whom she would relinquish that independence. The break with Gillot left her ill, but with a full sense of joy and affirmation of life. At the University of Zurich she applied herself to studies of comparative religion and philosophy, intellectual adventures that would prepare Lou to stand her ground with various distinguished minds. It also pleased her enormously that her fledgling, confessional poetry was being taken seriously. In time, health reasons forced her to seek a better climate southward and she drifted into a circle hosted by Malwida von Meysenbug, author of the best-selling and voluminous *Memoirs of an Idealist*. Her villa which overlooked Rome was a gathering place for devotees of philosophy and poetry; at *soirées* the tone of lectures and discussions was cultivated. She encouraged the exchange of cultural and spiritual knowledge within the bounds of strict propriety between the sexes; emancipation, she believed, could be achieved without abandoning societal conventions. There, Lou heard Paul Rée speak and was convinced that a friendship would suit them both. The son of a Pomeranian landowner, Rée interrupted his studies of law to volunteer for combat in the Franco-Prussian war, during which he was wounded; afterwards he changed his studies to philosophy and obtained a doctorate with a dissertation on Aristotle's ethics. He published a book of aphorisms, which solidified a friendship with Nietzsche and combined his knowledge of law and philosophy in a vast enterprise of tracking the genealogy of morals through the criminal codes of primitive and modern people. Conscience, he felt, is the cultural result of people becoming habituated to laws of prohibition and recognizing the utility of living in peace. Somewhat pessimistically he concluded that self-interest is the mainspring of man's animalistic and egotistic nature. Vanity makes man the vilest beast of prey, against which one must adopt a private code of behavior. Lou was fascinated by Rée's intellectual probings. Until then, her religious experiences had been variously personal, mystical, or rational. She had become disillusioned and had lost faith, yet the question of faith still troubled her, so that she welcomed a new approach through psychological analysis.

By accepting Lou's proposal that they live together as brother and sister and establish a cultural salon, Rée threw all caution to the winds and agreed to the sexless arrangement; like Gillot, Rée was to regret that idealistic move, and if Lou should have known better, her actions seemed unconcerned behind the guise of free self-development. Rumors of Lou's strange behavior reached her mother who wrote to Gillot, asking him to remind Lou of conventions and proprieties. Gillot did write, and his "girl" responded that she did not need advice but only the confidence of her former tutor. Rée, too, in a gesture of love and with his wish to spare Lou the tongues of gossips, sought the permission of Lou's mother to marry her daughter. Lou was furious when she heard about this and petulantly expressed little concern over what people might say about her behavior. The bizarre housekeeping was to continue for five years. But from the start a grim comedy of cross-purposes ensued. Lou confided to Rée her fantasy of creating a "holy trinity"—almost a parody of religious vision—that required the addition of a third person. Foolishly Rée took the bait, and without much reflection hit upon the idea of enlisting Nietzsche—who was seventeen years older than Lou—as a spiritual chaperone. Rée proposed a meeting, and Nietzsche replied with mock seriousness: "Greet that Russian girl for me, if that would serve any purpose: I am greedy for that species of soul. Indeed I seek such prey; I need her, in view of what I wish to do the next ten years. Marriage is an entirely different chapter; at most I could agree to a two-year marriage. . . ." His first words of greeting struck much too calculated a chivalric pose: "From what two stars have we fallen to meet here?" Flustered, Lou told him that she came from Zurich.

The projected trinity did not have much of a chance to survive on an astral plane. For Rée, who thought that he was being used to carry marriage proposals to Lou on behalf of Nietzsche, things proved intolerable. For Lou, matters proved exciting. She was flattered by the attention of Nietzsche, who signed a photograph for her styling himself as a "fugitive ex-professor of philosophy." He revised some of Lou's poetry, setting it to music, and in long, animated discussions treated her without condescension. Of the shared experiences, Nietzsche was to remember especially, "the most rapturous moment of my life, that I owe you." Vacationing near Orta in Italy, Lou and Nietzsche excused themselves from her mother and Rée and hiked up Monte Sacro. The coincidental symbolism of that name was inescapable. What transpired between the two supremely self-centered persons is not known, but the "Lou of Monte Sacro" lingered long in Nietzsche's memory, while Lou professed in her memoirs not being able to remember if she went so far as to kiss Nietzsche. Descending from the mount of mystery, Nietzsche expressed his hope that through his new-found alter ego, he might also find the person to help him toward his goals. For Rée the episode confirmed his own aphorism that all humans are equals in vanity and selfishness.

Lou, of course, had no permanent liaisons in mind. At Nietzsche's promptings, the trinity met again in Lucerne. Nietzsche, according to Lou, was in high spirits and contrived to have a picture taken of the three and arranged every last detail. Rée loathed the idea but allowed himself and Nietzsche to be posed pulling the shafts of a two-wheel cart. Lou was posed half-crouching on the cart, holding in her gloved left hand ropes tied

to the arms of the men and brandishing in her right hand a whip with a long lilac stalk. Lou and Rée show no amusement, though Lou kept the photo as a memento. When the photo was published shortly after, it proved to be a thorn, while it enhanced the notoriety of what surely was a grotesque situation.

Passionate non-marital intellectual and spiritual relationships fascinated Lou and Nietzsche theoretically, but in their own case recriminations and vitriolic hostilities by others soon broke up what could have remained a friendship; while it lasted, both sated their egos.

Nietzsche passionately admired and was stimulated by Lou's physicality and quickness of mind, but when he thought himself spurned he could lose control of his emotions and castigate her as a "she-monkey with false breasts, a pseudo-girl." His exasperation with Lou and his own sister and mother translated itself into ambivalent pronouncements on women in *Thus Spoke Zarathustra*, while Lou brought the reflections and perceptions gained through the Nietzsche encounter into her autobiographical novel *Im Kampf um Gott* (*A Struggle for God*, 1885). To protect the figures *à clef*, and probably with an eye toward the book's marketability, the young author chose the pseudonym of Henri Lou. The name Henri suspiciously resembled Hendrik Gillot's first name. In the novel's argumentations, Lou's heroine speaks out for intellectual and psychological equality for the sexes and against the imposed double standards of morality and the confinements of home and marriage.

Why Lou would wish to flirt continuously with psychological dangers is an unresolvable question, despite the efforts of biographers to unravel the mystery. While living with Rée in Berlin, Lou told him that she would continue to see an older man, Fred Charles Andreas, a brilliant and eccentric professor of Oriental philology and literatures, unless Rée were to object. Rée did not, possibly because he put trust in their eternal friendship. When she suddenly announced her engagement in November 1886, Rée sensed tragedy and quietly went out of her life. (He became a physician and immured himself in the provinces where he devoted his services primarily to the poor.) What Rée did not know was the account of Lou's turmoil, which she was to describe much later in her memoirs. Andreas was a passionate wooer who could not gain Lou's hand in marriage until in desperation he plunged a knife into his chest, escaping death by a fraction. Lou agreed to marriage, but again, as in her relationships with other men in her life, only upon her own terms. She would never again capitulate to forms of emotional blackmail. We also learn that Andreas Germanized his first name, Fred, to Friedrich, and Lou, addressing him as Fried or F., was able to imagine a surrogate marriage to Nietzsche and also imply its psychological impossibility.

Lou's sense of grotesque drama knew no limits and took no account of others' sensitivities. She wished her wedding to take place in the same Dutch church where she had been confirmed and with the ceremonies to be performed by Gillot. When he declined to follow Lou's scenario, she promised to take the wedding to St. Petersburg where, as her minister, Gillot would not be able to refuse. If Andreas took little satisfaction in these proceedings, he could take even less comfort in subsequent developments. Through Lou's disinclinations, the marriage was never consummated but remained one in name only for more than forty years. At the start, unresolved psychological problems lurked, probably centering on her inability to cut the ties with the memory of her father and hovering close to "incest dread." The problem, as H. F. Peters sees it, was partly compounded by Andreas' "violent attempts to subdue her, and partly in the fact that she saw in him not so much a husband as a father. All her life she remained her father's child. . . . Lou often refers to her husband as 'Alterchen,' the 'little old man,' an expression that shows the ambivalence of her feelings." Similarly, Rudolph Binion declares that by "making Andreas kneel with her before Gillot in Sandpoort, Lou meant to demote Andreas from an untouchable father-god. . . . With Fred she proved frigid." Aside from such conjectures, it was certain that she was unwilling to submit to what she felt was not only duress but also a violation of her independence. There were to be no sexual barriers between Lou and her lovers later on.

Until Andreas' death in 1930, her stays with him became more and more infrequent, despite intellectual affinities. Being financially independent of Andreas permitted Lou to travel constantly, at first with the support of her family and then through her own income from her writings—essays, reviews, novels, short stories. She encouraged Andreas to find a wifely substitute, and he did with a housekeeper who bore him children, one of whom later became a true daughter in Lou's old age. From the outset then, two strong wills in contention had come to an amicable agreement: no divorce; Lou was to be bound in name only, retaining her inner self-determination in every respect. Both were to be extraordinarily productive in their chosen ways, except that Andreas' major scholarly book was always in progress but never published.

In contact with all the mature men Lou admired, she learned a great deal. And so it was with Andreas, especially during the first two years while they lived in the suburbs of Berlin. They shared some interests and Andreas read to her and translated from the Norwegian the plays of Ibsen, often before the German translations appeared. She had become enormously attracted to the stage work of Ibsen because she instantly understood that Ibsen's characterizations of female figures reflected women's dilemmas in general and some of her own experiences in specifics. The problems of independence and emancipation as seen by Lou and Ibsen were rooted more in psychological situations than in obvious social and economic spheres.

In 1889 Lou met the leading persons of a newly-founded avant-gardist theater and literature group, somewhat like Antoine's Théâtre Libre in Paris. The group's call for a "free" stage was evident in its name, Die Frei Volksbühne, and it also published a journal *Die Freie Bühne* which urged a revolution of the human spirit and the socialization of the capitalistic system. Lou paid no attention to the political aspects, and fortunately neither did Otto Brahm, the director of the group's theater, which was to last two seasons. Because Ibsen's name at that time was anathema to the legitimate stage, the private Volksbühne—which drew its best actors from established troupes—decided on Ibsen's *Ghosts* for its opening anti-establishment salvo on September 29, 1889. The audience repeated the thunderous acclaim that had greeted the tearfully happy Ibsen two years earlier at another private performance in Berlin.

Lou attended rehearsals and wrote articles for *Die Freie Bühne*, championing the theatrical offerings of the group that also in-

cluded playwright Gerhart Hauptmann. All this, in addition to
the rumors and notoriety that linked her to an affair with Nietzsche, established for the vivacious Lou enthusiastic rapport with
the bohemian group. Undoubtedly she read Brahm's long
biographical and critical essay that eulogistically introduced
Ibsen to German audiences. Brahm had sought out Ibsen in Rome
and described him as a figure who would have stimulated Miche-
langelo's fantasy in modeling sculpture. The towering, lonely
and embattled figure of Ibsen was one that Brahm saw transformed into the heroes of the plays. "Each Ibsen figure is closely
scrutinized," wrote Brahm, "and achieves full existence; each
figure is individualized through distinctive character features
down to the smallest details." Lou would readily agree that
Ibsen's creations were lifelike figures rather than stage characters, an impression furthered by her Viennese friend Hugo von
Hofmannsthal in his essay on "The People in Ibsen's Dramas."
Like Lou, Hofmannsthal saw Ibsen's people as variations on
complex and richly modern types. Brahm, Lou, Hauptmann and
Hofmannsthal—among the Ibsenites—understood and felt
Ibsen's manner of creation.

II

CONFESSION AND RELEASE, as well as self-judgment, were the
motivations Ibsen ascribed to his creative impulse. During a
speech in 1874 to the students of Oslo, Ibsen said:

> . . . everything I have written I have lived through mentally. But no poet
> lives through anything in isolation. What he lives through all his country-
> men live through together with him. . . . Partly I have written about that
> which, only by glimpses and at my best moments, I have felt stirring vividly
> within me as something great and beautiful. . . . I have also written about
> that which to introspective contemplation appears as the dregs and sediment
> of one's own nature. . . . Nobody can present poetically that of which he has
> not had, to a certain degree at least at times, the model within himself. . . .
> A student has the same task as the poet: to make clear to himself, and thereby
> to others, the temporal and eternal questions which are astir in the age and in
> the community to which he belongs.

Six years later he wrote an equally noteworthy letter to Ludwig
Passarge, the German translator of *Peer Gynt*:

. . . Everything that I have written has the closest possible connection with what I have lived through . . . in every new poem or play I have aimed at my own spiritual emancipation and purification—for a man shares the responsibility and the guilt of the society to which he belongs. Hence I once wrote the following dedicatory lines in a copy of one of my books:
 To live *is to battle with fiends*
   that infest the brain and the heart.
 To write *is to hold a Last-Judgment*
   over one's self.

Observations about society and equally unsparing portrayals of his constant reappraisals form the vantage points in Ibsen's plays. If direct autobiography did not enter his work, then decidedly it was poetic truth which did.

Sudden turns of fortune marred the young Ibsen's life, which began in the Norwegian town of Skien, with its few thousand inhabitants. More than a hundred years before he was born in 1828, his ancestor Peter Ibsen helped to found a family that was to grow rich on commerce but declined into bankruptcy by 1836, forcing the Ibsens to move from a town home to a farm house. Whether these circumstances or guilt feelings of the young Ibsen about his escapades resulted in his break with—and even antipathy for—his father and family is not known; but except for one visit and sporadic correspondence with his younger sister, after he was sixteen years old, he was never to have close contact with them. As a pharmacy apprentice in Grimsted, another provincial southern town, he suffered further poverty, loneliness, and neglect. Seeking an outlet for his restlessness, he took to painting scenes of the harbor town, with passable results. But though his socializing was infrequent, it was not nearly as innocuous as his painting. He fathered a son by a domestic servant ten years older than himself and soberly fulfilled legal obligations for child support during fourteen years, but assumed no other paternal responsibilities. No autobiographical sources tell us of any struggles with his conscience, yet he had not been unable to ignore the uproar that ensued at the scandalizing disclosure of his social impropriety. "Conventional morality," Ibsen discovered for himself, proved to be public disapproval of private double standards.

Solitary persons often take to such lonely preoccupations as writing. The young Ibsen wrote poems and plays which filled his time and were of fledgling worth. He also harbored thoughts of becoming a doctor and moved to Christiania (now Oslo) to prime for matriculation at the university. All these ambitions came to naught. Instead, he began writing articles for a radical weekly and reviewing theatrical productions for a student paper. The die was cast finally when he received a call from the Norwegian theater in Bergen to assume the modest post of assistant stage manager. During the years 1851 to 1857 he had a chance to study first-hand the flourishing theaters in Danish cities and in Germany. With that experience, he was ready to assume a directorship of Christiania's new Norwegian Theater, all the while writing for the stage in attempting to satisfy audience taste for nationalistic fare: historical dramas, plays that drew on folk material and medieval sources.

As a theatrical producer Ibsen managed his craft well, but generally paid little attention to the actors; he treated actresses with aloof amiability and kindness, and he shirked giving necessary criticism. He did some respectable courting, but as stories have it, he ran like a hare when an officious father confronted him, leaving the girl alone to brave the storm. It was love at first sight again, when he met Susanna, the step-daughter of a well-known author, Marie Thoresen. His impecunious lot, however, forced postponement of marriage until 1858. From varying accounts, Susanna was an extremely efficient manager of household affairs, attuned to and generally tolerant of her husband's fluctuating moods and his controlled but explosive temperament, described as that of a self-styled Old Testament prophet. She was protective of his working hours to the point of reducing their socializing to a minimum, and also preventing him from being dragged away by "bad" cronies. Above all, she had an abiding faith in his genius.

Otto Brahm thought that from Ibsen's observations about his own courtship days and the early years of marriage there floated thinly disguised figures into his play *Love's Comedy* of 1862:

> . . . *Ibsen had to observe from his experiences what had previously amused and irritated him while observing others: the dreamy bliss of a first love yielded to solemnly proclaimed engagement, for which everyone was called upon to be a witness; well-wishers and aunts flocked, tongues censoriously clucked and carried gossip throughout the town. And then the satiric-*

minded writer looked about him and his breast was filled with bitterness and doubt when he compared the beginning and end-point, love and marriage. Love seemed to him poetic, marriage prosaic. Love seemed to him holy, marriage comic. Love makes one free and releases the inmost and best in people; marriage enchains. . . .

Ibsen's marriage is veiled in privacy. But Brahm's view that Ibsen chafed at being a husband, at the start, is correct. We know from Ibsen's son that he would rather have escaped, but also that without Susanna he would have been disconsolate; she was a source of his strength. Although the transference or metamorphosis of autobiography into fiction is much more complex than Brahm pictures it, he accurately notes that Ibsen abandoned historical sources and began to draw more freely on experience and the contemporaneous scene.

Despite the closeness to his family, Ibsen needed other outlets. To Emilie Bardach he wrote,

I receive your letter with a thousand thanks—and have read it, and read it again. Here I sit as usual at my desk, and would gladly work, but cannot do so.

My imagination is ragingly at work, but is always straying to where in working hours it should not. I cannot keep down the memories of the summer, neither do I want to. The things we have lived through I live again and again—and still again. To make of them a poem is for the time being impossible. . . . (October 15, 1889)

The idea of "poetry" as expressive of what has been "lived through" is thematic in Ibsen's thoughts.

He asked if it was stupidity or madness, or both, that precipitated a brief but emotionally lasting experience, an "unattainable . . . unfathomable reality," a summer that "was the happiest, the most beautiful in my whole life." On the back of a photograph the young admirer had sought from the old celebrity, he wrote, "To the May sun of a September life." In the first flush of the sudden romance, he idealized Emilie as "a lovely creature of the summer, dear Princess, I have known you, as a being of the season of butterflies and wild flowers. How I should like to see you as you are in winter! . . . Quick, poised like a bird, gracious in velvet and furs . . . at the theater, leaning back, a tired look in your mysterious eyes. . . ."

At sixty Ibsen could not have pursued any "mad" longings

for Emilie without rupturing his family responsibilities, risking widespread personal scandal, and without conscious or unconscious fear of relating physically and emotionally to someone less than half his age, although she was receptive to what appeared to her inexperienced mind to be Ibsen's "volcanic passion." Closer at hand than Emilie in Vienna was another young girl in Munich, Helene Raff, who sought his company and affection. Long after Ibsen's death Helene shed light on Ibsen's romances:

> I must admit, however, that because of this need of the aging man who yearns for youth, he has at times struck a too-devoted tone face to face with young women and that his wife was offended because she thought such things not in conformity with his dignity. For this reason she assumed at times a harsh attitude to such matters.

Helene also speculated that "Ibsen's relations with young girls had in them nothing whatever of infidelity in the usual sense of the term, but arose solely from the needs of his imagination; as he himself said, he sought out youth because he needed it for his poetic production." If this was the case, then an extraordinary transmutation of fact occurred when Ibsen, two months after his farewell letter to Emilie, was reported to have told Julius Elias, a literary historian, that he had met a remarkable Viennese girl, "a demonic little wrecker . . . a little bird of prey" who wanted to lure husbands away from their wives. It surely was wrong to proclaim virtuously that Emilie did not succeed in her designs on him, and in the next breath to boast that "I got hold of her—for my play," namely, *The Master Builder* with its destructively perverse young Hilde Wangel who drove Solness, a strong Ibsen self-image, to madness, while the wife, Aline Solness, has some of Susanna's features.* On the other hand, he may have spoken in the guise of the artist rather than strictly autobiographically.

––––––––––

*Lou felt betrayed by Ibsen's pessimistic, autobiographical tone in *The Master Builder* and deplored the loss of Ibsen's faith in the idealistic strivings of unique individuals. In her review of a stage performance in 1893, Lou thought that the problem was not with Hilde but with Solness' hypnotic will to dominate, a kind of self-determination "at the expense of others." Lou's intuitive grasp of that feature of Ibsen's unconscious self-portrayal was borne out by Emilie Bardach when in 1927, twenty-one years after Ibsen's death, she revealed a diary entry made on the heels of a disturbing rendezvous with the playwright: "He means to possess me. This is his absolute will. He intends to overcome all obstacles."

In the sketchy accounts we have of Ibsen's "summer madness," we gather that he wanted to understand every facet of Emilie Bardach's young personality, as well as to use her as a mirror for his aroused emotions; he encouraged her to give him all the personal details of her life. "A man," Ibsen said, "is easy to study, but one never fully understands a woman. They are a sea which none can fathom." Nevertheless, he set himself to fathom the mystery of women, the psychology of love and will and subterranean drives, within the contexts and constraints of society. The metaphor of sea or water remained central for Hedwig, Rebecca, Ellida. Notes for his plays show how totally he viewed and lived with his creations until they came alive onstage. Just as he had given concentrated attention to people's experiences, he reminded actors to "observe the life that is going on around you and to present a real and living human being."

About the lives and lot of modern women, he came to explicit and sympathetic conclusions:

> There are two kinds of moral laws, two kinds of conscience, one for men and one quite different, for women. They don't understand each other; but in practical life, woman is judged by masculine law, as though she weren't a woman but a man.
>
> A woman cannot be herself in modern society. It is an exclusively male society, with laws made by men and with prosecutors and judges who assess feminine conduct from a masculine standpoint.
>
> . . . A mother in modern society, like certain insects, retires and dies once she has done her duty by propagating the race. . . . Everything must be borne alone. (From Ibsen's "Notes for a Modern Tragedy," Rome, October 19, 1878)

He was outlining the fate of Nora had she stayed in her doll's house, but neither in fact or fiction did he propose emancipation as a solution. The choice, he knew, rests with individuals, and the consequences depend upon the reaction of a male-dominated society. In Ibsen's time Laura Kieler, Nora's live prototype, suffered devastating consequences. Beyond that specific instance, however, the impact of the play was like dynamite thrown into conventional marital codes, opening the way to social debates.

What however was bold and refreshing about Ibsen in his role as a public figure and celebrity was his challenging question: "Is there anyone . . . who dares to assert that our ladies [of the Scandinavian library association] are inferior to us in culture, or intelligence, or knowledge, or artistic talent?" Several days later he noted that women can be just as stupid as men. Such even-handed assertions made clear his view that women are persons and not "dolls."

He was being perfectly in character when he told the Norwegian Women's Rights League that whatever he wrote "has been without conscious thought of making propaganda," and that he was "more poet and less social philosopher." The problem of women's rights, along with those of others, needs solution but it was his main task to "describe" humanity. It should be the task of politics to make a society free. As for "free" Norway, he thought it to be peopled by unfree women *and* unfree men. That point is implicit in *A Doll's House,* and in Lou Salomé's reading of the play, she clearly understood that Helmer is trapped by convention as much as Nora.

III

IBSEN HAD HIS TRUMPETERS all over Europe; among the earliest were Brandes in Scandinavia, Brahm and Salomé in Germany, and Shaw in England. Ibsen returned to Christiania in 1891; he was lionized and became a tourist attraction, a celebrity. In that same year Lou Salomé's *Henrik Ibsens Frauen-Gestalten* and Shaw's *The Quintessence of Ibsenism,* each in its own way, helped to gain attention for the Norwegian dramatist. Both took into account audiences which barely knew Ibsen and therefore they did more "telling the story of the plays" than what we might find necessary; but "telling" is also interpretation and exposition of Ibsen's plays. Both avoided practicing their critical abilities upon the body of Ibsen's work; instead, they closely followed Ibsen's technique of slowly revealing the lives of men and women corseted by societal conventions and their responses to demands for conformity, duties and responsibilities. Shaw reminded readers "who may think that I have forgotten to reduce Ibsenism to a formula for them, that its quintessence is that there is no formula." Lou would agree and add that Ibsen was a master of improvising upon basic human relationships.

When Lou wrote her interpretations of Ibsen's six plays that center on women's interests, it was some twenty-one years before her professional association with Freud and before she became his "dear inexhaustible friend." Just as Freud pointed out in his introductory lectures to psychoanalysis that the validation of his theories rested upon each individual's personal insights into his own life, Lou measured the truth and plausibility of Ibsen's characterization in terms of her experiences and emotional dilemmas. As we have seen, Lou's family constellations, father-figures, lovers, husband-in-name, ministers, and the rebellion against social conformities were complicated and extraordinarily deep and convoluted. She wrote not out of a need for "self-healing" but out of a need to clarify outer societal relationships and dark inner subtleties. If her subjectivity comes through in the obvious prejudices she harbors for and against certain of Ibsen's personages, they do not interfere with her intuitive and intellectual appreciation of Ibsen's artistry.

The question of whether or not a male writer could portray the female psyche in its significant dimensions did not seem to enter Lou's mind, possibly because she found no false notes in Ibsen's characterizations and motivations socially and emotionally. Indeed, she saw that women and men, though under different constraints, were faced with similar problems of love, assertion of individual will, ethics, social commitments, emancipation from stifling conventions, inherited morality, and confusion of identity. Both could either betray or surmount the forces and drives within.

Lou's book *Henrik Ibsens Frauen-Gestalten* was translated and published in Norwegian in 1893 by her Berlin neighbor and friend Hulda Garborg, with an introduction by her husband Arne Garborg, but since then one must scour the literature to find mention or discussion of it. Writing from a defensively pro-Nietzschean bias, Binion sees Lou as a case study of a devious and "wayward" disciple:

> Though Lou's Ibsen book was extravagantly acclaimed in its time,* its big talk about ideals, and about sacrifice for ideals or for want of them—rings false in ours.** It was overwritten besides, with an excess of metaphor. And

---

*Ibsen himself saluted it affably in a letter of 5/11/1891 to the author— headed "Dear Sir"!
**But even forty years afterwards Meyer-Benfey (Heinrich M-B, "Lou Andreas-Salomé," *Die Frau*, February 1931: 304–07) called it "doubtless the most wonderful book ever written on Ibsen." (Binion, *Frau Lou*, p. 146)

*résumés make up far too much of it—though they do incidentally show to
how great an extent "the on-stage Ibsen drama constitutes as it were only a
last act, sums up a long development" . . . which was one ground of Lou's
affinity for Ibsen: she too considered even the most spontaneous-seeming
conduct to have its complicated prehistory. Finally, she discussed neither
Ibsen's plays nor even his characterizations, but his characters themselves,
quite as if they were real people: her original sin.*

If it is an "original sin" (according to Binion) to regard Ibsen's
"characters themselves, quite as if they were real people," Lou is
in good company indeed. Countless theater audiences, directors
from Brahm on, as well as a long line of theater critics from Shaw
to Eric Bentley treated Ibsen's creations on stage as if they were
real individuals, persons, or figures. Ibsen has described the
gestation of characters in his mind, who emerged as individuals
only after he had plunged into their interior "to penetrate into the
last wrinkle" of their soul, ascertained the aspects of their humanity, and then visualized their exteriors "down to the last
button"—their walk, voice, and bearing. The measure of Ibsen's
success lies in audiences' response to Ibsen's efforts to make his
figures believable humans and credible persons.

Lou's retelling of six female-dominated plays through *description*, renders an impressionistic *interpretation* of the plays. That
technique, even if the aim is understood, risks the charge of
overwriting with an excess of metaphor. No doubt Lou's style
contains rhetorical excess, painting with words intended to affect
the reader, which frequently circles around a point until she
decides to zero in with an incisive conclusion. The proliferation of
metaphors in Lou's Ibsen essays may seem self-indulgent, except
that one must realize that she is playing with variations upon
those metaphors through which Ibsen himself shapes the mood
and substance of his plays; the metaphors and images are equiv-
alents for human emotions and psychological behavior. In Lou's
writing, we find intuitive thoughts that slowly unfold and imitate
the course of her meditation and probing. Her language is emotional yet philosophical, free from the clinical and analytic ter-
minology she was later to acquire in the school of Freud and also
free of the modern critical cant that the value of criticism increases
as it approaches unintelligibility.

Lou realized uniquely, through her own love for poetry, that

Ibsen's dramas contain strong poetic fibers that give them thematic unity and an organic mood: visual representations complement the symbolic actions of the plays; stage props become integral links from past to present; references to nature's scenes and seasons in the talk of the individuals forge links from the personal past or "prehistory" to the present or retributive, epiphanal moment; simile and metaphor are expressive of psychological dilemmas; indirections give clues to inner emotions, and the proverbial is the protective language of conscience and the unconscious. With such approaches to Ibsen's plays, Lou was far ahead of her time, and unfortunately her interpretations dropped out of sight.

Lou's essays are especially valuable in that they represent the view of the first woman writer to tell us if Ibsen came at all close in his objective to capture the dimensions of the female psyche. Not until our time have other female critics, theater directors, and generalists taken a searching look at Ibsen's creations. Of course, there is no unanimity of response, there are even sharp differences; but altogether there appears to be a consensus about the psychological validity of his perception of women in all their aspects*: the mother image, daughter role, sister relationship, fiancée or mistress, wife, and interloper.

Just as Ibsen's experiences and reflections shaped his plays, so did Lou's reactions to them. Remarkable in the biographies of Lou and Ibsen is the coincidence on many points of their personality and responses to conventions. There is no critical jargon in Lou's writing about Ibsen's female figures; instead, she sees them and the situations within which they move as absolutely organic. And so, her distinctive interpretations rest on perceiving the minutiae that give Ibsen's plays their effective unity.

IV

THE IDEA OF WOMAN'S CAPTIVITY within her personality, family, and society is central to Ibsen's metaphors and imagery. Lou

---

*Cf. Clela Allphin, *Women in the Plays of Ibsen* (New York: Revisionist Press, 1975), and Elenore Lester, "Ibsen's Unliberated Heroines," *Scandinavian Review* (December 1978).

selects the once-wild duck as a central "captive" analogy and introduces her essays on Ibsen's female figures with an encompassing "Fable." The duck then becomes symbolic of Nora whose self-realization allows her to wing away from husband and children. Mrs. Alving is like a helpless duck languishing in captivity. Hedwig, maimed, perishes in the attic. Rebecca invades the attic world and causes havoc among the other wildlife. Ellida is tamed by kindness and a recognition of her right to self-definition and determination. Hedda reveals herself to be a purposeless, cowardly, and destructive creature who fails to realize her free-born nature.

Lou's "Fable" is too elaborate and overextends metaphor into conceit (although it keeps the images of birds and captivity in Ibsen's poetry and plays), so that readers probably would be better served by first absorbing the essays. In this translation of Lou's book, it has been put in the place of an epilogue.

For each play Lou discussed, she chose prefatory lines that in a nutshell signified to her the main thrust of the human drama through the words of a main figure. For *A Doll's House*, she chose Nora's hope-filled words, "After all, it is splendid to be waiting for a wonderful thing to happen." That wonderful thing would have been for her husband to appreciate and understand her sacrifices, to stand by her, and finally to accord her equality within the family.

Subjectively, the dimensions of marriage were of concern to Lou, and she notes the ironic reversals that Ibsen suggests in the two marriages: Helmer and Nora, Krogstad and Mrs. Linde. Of course, there is the prehistory that also intrigued Lou as Nora is transformed from a father-worshipping bride to a person who silently shoulders financial burdens and begins to feel that she possesses "a man's strength." When that happens she is able to break the hold of godlike father figures. Nora, as Lou, rebelled at being submissive to the blandishment that one must avoid the potential censure of society. Nora, unlike Helmer, will not be taken in by the argument of "What will people say?" She courageously faces the task of self-education. Nora becomes not the prototype of the New Woman, but the example of a new human being. So much attention has been paid to Nora during the play's stage history that only a few critics have noted what

Lou said initially about Helmer's pathetic situation: he too is a captive who has failed to see that the objects of his pleasure have "pinions" on their shoulders "capable of lifting him out of his narrow doll house"; he too needs to be emancipated.

Lou's views portray a Nora who leaves not so much out of defiance and despair but because of her dispelled illusions: Nora's husband, who failed to dignify her as a marriage partner, no longer is a god or father figure but a confused male caught in conventionality.

Lou's interpretation of *Ghosts* is as clearly phrased as Ibsen's natural language of the play in which he had finally achieved mastery of "the far more difficult art of prose" as spoken in real life. But unlike Ibsen who owlishly refused to reveal whether or not Mrs. Alving would honor her oath and give her debilitated son the morphium powder he had demanded, or unlike critics who decidedly said that she would not, Lou was certain that the mother will give her son the liberating poison—she will do it with a symbolic gesture: she will be compelled to destroy with her own hand what she has built up on a false foundation, just as she had to disavow and recant what she had bred and defended in her involuntary mistakes." Lou saw that gesture not as part of a theatrical debate about mercy killing which—like the topics of incest and venereal disease—shocked many of her contemporaries, but she regarded it as a culmination of Mrs. Alving's new integrity.

Lou observes in Mrs. Alving a grand bearing and "the superlative trait of her womanly nature to gather all personal agony and experience into silent understanding and perception." The peak of the play, for Lou, is reached when Helene Alving perceives the pattern of her experience: "Now I see what happened. . . . And now I can speak out. And yet, no ideals will collapse." At that point she decides to liberate Oswald from his guilty self-reproaches by telling the truth about his father and correcting the false façade she had deliberately created. Now she understands objectively why as a bride she failed Alving and herself.

Helene's life is a continual transformation from one state to another: initial unpreparedness for marriage; disillusionment as a bride; the victim of a marriage to an experienced sensualist into

whose fantasies she enters desperately to keep him ensnared in
their home; the assertion of her will and tyrannical takeover of all
family responsibilities; and finally, her shattered anticipation of
happiness through a surviving son. But Lou's imagination is also
caught by the metaphors and images that Ibsen has subtly pro-
vided, so that she makes a comparison no one else has made:
Helene "could not raise against her own marriage Nora's reproach that marriage had kept her as tightly closed as an unripe
bud. Forcefully and ruthlessly Helene's buds are torn open, not
by the natural light rays of the sun but through the disgusting
influence of a repulsive and unnerving power that resembles a
crawling, devouring worm which opens up buds only to defoliate
them." Lou's powerful accentuation reflects not only Ibsen's
metaphorical suggestiveness but also her personal attunement to
the female psyche and its fears and fantasies. The social and
psychological implications of the male worm powerfully takes us
into Helene's mind. By the same token, the images of defoliation
in nature and defloration in humans are not Lou's inventions;
they exist in the descriptions embedded in Ibsen's plays.

The sun and sunlight in Oswald's paintings and the brooding
mists that cannot be pierced and that lie heavily over the Alving
house are allusions as effective as the fire that produces the ashes
which spread over Mrs. Alving's life. Pastor Manders remarks
how much her son Oswald resembles his father, and critics have
pointed to the return of the ghosts of the past through Oswald,
but Lou believes that Mrs. Alving's tragic past relationship to her
deceased husband has been transformed through her son, allowing her to forgive much of the past and giving her the courage to
confess a great deal to Oswald. The play is not a thesis-like
exposure of the hollowness of bourgeois family life and conventions as commonly explained by critics, but as viewed by Lou the
play is about one woman's growth of confidence and willingness
to expose the corruption she has tolerated by adhering to false
ideals. Helene has resolved to tell the non-idealistic truth in order
to save her son and to bring tranquillity to her own mind.

It is as if Helene had soared to the snow-peaks visible from
her windows. At the play's ending, the appearance of the sun is
far from being a cloying invention. Ironically it is the sun, in fact
and image, that has never warmed her sexual life and it

represents the joy of life that her son had vainly sought. Though Mrs. Alving remains in "the depths and under the shadows," Lou also envisions that the transformation in her life leads toward the sun.

Mrs. Alving was deliberately chosen by Ibsen to be Nora's successor. Where Nora abandoned a doll's house and an irreconcilable marriage, Helene stayed and submitted— responsibly or irresponsibly—with tragic consequences.

Ibsen described *The Wild Duck* as a tragi-comedy, suggesting that audiences and readers understand the figures of the play through dual perspectives. Lou seemed not very much concerned with technical designations, but rather sees the spine or main thrust of the play in that the little Hedwig "died for the love" of Helmer. Danger lurks for Hedwig, says Lou, because her love and admiration for her father challenge Hjalmar not to shame her expectations. Hedwig takes in deadly earnest "what merely are empty phrases and grand rhetoric," and in that sham environment she does something real. Hedwig shoots herself because, as she had declared earlier, she would always stay and help mother and father. At the point when Hjalmar sarcastically implies that Hedwig would choose Werle's wealth rather than remain in poverty with him, Hedwig's shot gives *her* answer: she would stay. She also joyously responded to Gregers' challenge for a "sacrifice." Lou's reading is valid and satisfying because in the sweep of the play there are multiple motivations that lead to Hedwig's self-sacrifice rather than a singular "over-interpretation"* of what the adults are saying.

In Hedwig's "trustful nestling close to her father and in her devoted love for him," Lou sees a transitional figure between the pairs of Nora and Mrs. Alving and the later Ellida, "the lady of the sea," and Hedda Gabler. The former erroneously glorify their lovers and must gain freedom while the latter idealize their own love and then sacrifice themselves. Since Lou calls Hedwig "a tiny figuration of poetry," she traces her presence throughout the play with equally poetic feeling; but on the other hand, she does not fail to pick up the symbolism and realism of the swamp odor

---

*Cf. Mary McCarthy, "The Will and Testament of Ibsen," *Sights and Spectacles* (New York: Farrar, Straus & Cudahy, 1956).

created by Gregers' ineptness in lighting the stove, which fouls the atmosphere of the Ekdal home, nor does she resist the wry but accurate comment that Hjalmar "was never accustomed to high style and was not about now to don a tragic toga; he was more comfortably habituated to a shabby housejacket."

In Lou's concentration on the female figures in Ibsen's plays, she did not permit her knowledge of Ibsen's biography to interfere with her interpretation of the plays. Ibsen expressed his concern for the proper casting, setting, and lighting for the play; he insisted that "in both the ensemble acting and in the stage setting, this play demands truth to nature and a touch of reality in every respect. The lighting too has its significance. . . ." Lou is attentive to everything from directions for stage lighting to descriptions of gestures. Lou understood that the small, involuntary actions were the surface manifestations of underlying psychological patterns which need to be brought into sharp relief for readers, a task similar in nature to Freud's exposure of "the psychopathology of everyday life."

Lou's essay on Ibsen's *Rosmersholm* is somewhat rambly and discursive because she slowly unravels the varieties of strands woven into the tightly-knit play. After revisiting Norway in 1886, Ibsen had given a great deal of thought to that country's political situation and societal transformations. Not impersonal forces, he thought, would bring about changes but the "nobility of mind and will" which compose human character and purpose would have a liberating influence. He further wanted the play *Rosmersholm* to deal "with the struggle which all serious-minded humans have to wage with themselves in order to bring their lives into harmony with their convictions." In people's relation to one another, individual spiritual functions, moral consciousness or conscience develop at a different pace and often as a result of inner conflicts and outer drama. Such abstractions were important, notes Ibsen. But he went on to say, "not until I had come to a distinct understanding of my experiences and had drawn my conclusions could I transform my thoughts into a work of fiction." Lou's essay on *Rosmersholm* anatomizes the complex sinews of what Ibsen called each "true and living figure" on stage. It also seemed as if Lou as an interpreter heard and followed Ibsen's demand upon actors and actresses that they bring their "own observation of real life" into their roles.

Lou sees the spine of the play in the reversal of opposing values by Rosmer and Rebecca so that their destiny tragically converges: "now we two are one." When Rosmer and Rebecca alter their original philosophies of life, they find no satisfying substitutes and they incur the loss of self. What ennobles may ironically also destroy. The influence of one person upon another's mind may resemble infection which leads to debilitation rather than a cure.

Otto Rank in 1922 saw the oedipal scenario at work in literature and legend in his study of *Das Inzest-Motiv in Dichtung und Sage*. He noted that the incestuous relation between the knowing father, Doctor West, and the unknowing Rebecca was shrouded by Ibsen in muted tones to represent the repressed and lifelike facts embodied in the prehistory of the play. Rank makes the observation that in Ibsen's *Rosmersholm* "the mighty inner resistances prevent a distinct expression of unconscious motivations."

Freud orchestrated Rank's brief observations into a significantly deeper interpretation: Rebecca's unconscious incest guilt underlies her conscious renunciation of happiness. He justified treating Ibsen's Rebecca West as if she were a living person who is directed by the most critical intelligence. Moreover, Freud saw a complete agreement between literature and clinical experience. Like Rank, he suggested that the incest situation had to remain concealed from the viewer's or reader's perception, "otherwise serious resistances" could have endangered the effect of the play. In his essay "Some Character Types" (1916), Freud makes these points:

> The enigma of Rebecca's behavior is susceptible of only one solution. The news that Dr. West was her father is the heaviest blow that could strike her, for she was not only his adopted daughter but had been his mistress. . . . She cannot have had anything else on her mind but this love-affair when she accounted for her final rejection of Rosmer on the ground that she had a past which made her unworthy to be his wife . . . this past must seem to her the most serious obstacle to their union—the more serious crime [when compared with the responsibility for driving Beate to suicide].

By the time Freud wrote the essay, Lou had become a devoted disciple and colleague, but their correspondence shows no knowledge on his part of the essay on *Rosmersholm* she had written some twenty-five years earlier, nor is there any indication of what Lou thought of Freud's essay. Lou ascribed Rebecca's rejection of Rosmer's marriage proposal to the impact of Beate's "ghost," the revenge of Beate; at the same time, Rebecca has experienced a weakened and alienated self that was "infected" by the debilitating insistence of Rosmer's tortured imagination, and his loss of faith in her though not his dependence upon her. Lou saw Rebecca as a person incapable of remorse but succumbing to the terror of Beate's ghost. In her youth, she was a creature as free and wild as the untrammeled natural environment of rugged land and sea, but the hothouse atmosphere at Rosmersholm changed and depressed her personality: the sleek beast of prey became dispiritedly domesticated. Not only did her relationship with Dr. West seem to leave no scar on her psyche as his daughter in name but she also uninhibitedly cared for him until his death. Freud emphasized the acquisition by Rebecca of "a sense of guilt which debars her from enjoyment" and prevents her from accepting Rosmer's marriage proposal, and Freud underscored the point that her professed motivations and "confessions" hide the basic one of incest-guilt. Lou instead sees the pivot of Rebecca's experience to be in the idealistic-seeming but fatal inversion of her values.

Freud, in a letter of October 28, 1917, reacted to a friendly challenge to his views by Georg Groddeck (dubbed "the wild man of psychoanalysis"):

> Dear esteemed colleague,
> . . . Your interesting observations and analysis of Rosmersholm has prompted me to read the play once again and to discuss it with my sole assistant, Dr. Hanns Sachs. We are of one mind not to yield to your view. Everything seems to us to point against the idea that Rebecca West's confession is fictive. Sachs believes that otherwise the life-nerve of the play would be severed. . . . Rosmer does put behind him his wife's suicide. His impotence is certainly discernible, but Ibsen has not connected it or made it the backbone of the play. . . .

A month later Groddeck replied:

> . . . I am curious as to how you explain that Rebecca overhears the conversation between Rosmer and Kroll and that Kroll gives her to understand that he knows who has written the anonymous letters. Ibsen is much too meticulous in his craft for anything to occur arbitrarily. I have found that after every reading of Ibsen's work one is confronted with new problems—esthetic and psychoanalytical. During the past several years, I have gained the impres-

sion that Ibsen has outwitted mankind in the most astonishing ways. Nora, specifically, is a case in point. That supposed proponent of women's rights lies in the same fashion as one is accustomed to hear lies in lecture halls. She holds tête à tête talks with her husband when he is obviously drunk, talks that would only be justified under quite other circumstances. Here the audience is mocked terribly and has fallen completely into a trap.

It is quite similar with The Master Builder, The Wild Duck, and above all Rosmersholm. The living nerve of the play, in my opinion, is thereby not affected but provides a new light in which pathos becomes ironic pathos. As soon as one sees the incongruity between means and results in Ibsen's work, one notices that he has not written middle-class dramas but comedies. I believe it altogether possible that he was fully aware of that and knew the silent laughter of the ironist. It is tragic irony that a woman as magnificent as Rebecca is so thoroughly devastated by the Rosmersholm milieu and by a person of ostensible "nobility."

Groddeck gives voice to the indignant feeling of some viewers that the full-blooded Rebecca should have been incapacitated by so lackluster a figure as Rosmer. He also discerned the strong element of irony that modern critics have since discovered in the play.

Lou no doubt would have accepted the psychoanalytic view that Rebecca replays the oedipal drama of her childhood by attempting to displace the rival mother figure Beate (or her own mother) and to marry Rosmer (the father figure who replaces Dr. West). She might not have agreed in 1916 that Rebecca admits to the *explicit* crime of driving Beate to suicide only in order to cover up the *implicit* or cardinal crime of incest. Before coming into Freud's psychoanalytic circle, her interpretations were not channeled into any specialized form. Lou placed great emphasis on the superstition-laden atmosphere of Rosmersholm as personified by the housekeeper who expressed her fear that the dead clutch at the living, a fear strongly verbalized also by Rebecca. Like Shaw, whose writings Lou did not know, she accepted the theme of Rebecca's fatal "conversion" that prompted her self-sacrifice and her dual suicide-wedding with Rosmer for the sake of spiritual fellowship. The psychological turning point, as Lou understood it, was the strange and dizzying feeling that stirs Rebecca: "Ever so slowly it came"—a capitulation to Rosmer's weakness and "morality," and an admiration for his "inner nobility."

The themes and figures in Ibsen's lustrous drama *The Lady of the Sea* enmeshed Lou's emotions and thoughts. Its heroine, Ellida, brought back Lou's own intense dream life—and the dangers of the life of the imagination—that had characterized her adolescence. If serious literature elicits response and encourages identification by readers and viewers, Lou's participating subjectively bears out that relationship. Perhaps envy and admiration went into her observation of the life-like evolving and maturing of Ellida and her husband, Dr. Wangel, toward a "true" marriage. She felt that her husband Andreas' obsessive claims upon her prevented him from willingly granting her the freedom which Dr. Wangel, through turmoil and sympathy, extended to his wife Ellida. Lou, depressed to the point of committing double suicide with Andreas—an uncanny variation of the Rebecca-Rosmer situation—finally wrenched herself free and pursued her own life outside of Andreas' attic world and immersed herself in experiences which he adamantly refused to hear about. Lou did dedicate the Ibsen book to Andreas ("Mein Mann"), but for authorial purposes assertively let her maiden name stand in all her published work. In her correspondence with Freud, however, she observed conventions and signed her name "Lou Andreas," while he addressed her as "Frau Lou."

And so, the personal motivations are quite obvious when Lou is prompted to say of Nora that "not for the sake of liberty does Nora wish to free herself, but only for the purpose of discovering her full resources . . . as a fully conscious human being." For the same reason, Lou idealizes Ellida's discovery of the possibilities of a marriage in which freedom, voluntary responsibilities, and mutual growth converge. Ellida and a foreign seaman pledge a troth. He disappears at sea, haunts her, and returns as the Stranger to claim her, although by then she is married to Dr. Wangel with whom *she* lives almost as a stranger. In tracing the development of *The Lady from the Sea,* Lou pays attention to the increasing points of suspense and intensity as Ellida, the conflicted wife, progressively gains new insights that are expressed through variations on a refrain: "Wangel, save me" . . . "Save me from that man" (the Stranger) . . . "Oh, Wangel! Save me from myself!" This is no mere tautology; the last outcry is a necessary climactic "self-perception" that leads to her balanced reconciliation—a happy ending which is not saccharine. The need to be "saved from one's self" has an implication that Lou could not face in her own mirror.

Shaw was of the opinion that the "subject of *The Lady from the Sea* is the most poetic fancy imaginable." That view had been anticipated by Lou's interpretation in which she mixes rhetoric and poetic prose with abandon and, albeit, some repetition. Beyond that, however, she enthusiastically notes "how thoroughly and inwardly Ibsen formulates the psychic problems." As has been discovered by the biographer-critic Halvdan Koht, Ellida derives from the pagan name of a ship Ellide in the *Saga of Frithiof the Bold* in which the ship is given human characteristics as it struggles against the powerful trolls of the sea; these supernatural creatures of folklore seek to drag Ellide down to the depths. In Ibsen's lengthy notes preparatory to writing the play, we find many of the strange thought associations and speculating moods of Ellida, as well as her objects of attraction and fantasies:

> The sea's magnetic power. The longing for the sea. Human beings akin to the sea. Bound by the sea. Dependent on the sea. One species of fish is a vital link in the chain of evolution. Do rudiments of it still reside in the human mind? . . .
>
> Images of the teeming life of the sea and of "what is lost for ever." . . . The sea operates a power over one's moods, it works like a will. The sea can hypnotize. The great mystery is the dependence of the human will on that which is will-less. . . . She has come from the sea . . . secretly engaged to the young, carefree ship's mate. . . . At heart, in her instincts—he is the one with whom she is living in marriage. . . .

Although Lou did not know of these Ibsen notes, her interpretation of *The Lady from the Sea* surely demonstrates how well Ibsen has concretized their ideas in the figures of the play and how well Lou tuned in to the "psychic" dimensions of Ellida's inner life and growth. Through Lou's essay we feel that the living and experiencing women take precedence over whatever didactic conclusions may be drawn from the play. Particularly perceptive is Lou's description of Ellida's mode of thinking in images: the actual is visualized in dreamlike states and becomes dissolved, so that only when reality changes her inner image of the Stranger does she see life in focus.

But there appears to be a sequel. Subsequent to the publication of Lou's book she wrote a long review of a later Ibsen play, which was included in the Norwegian translation. In that review she said:

> *Hilde Wangel is the youngest stepdaughter of "the lady from the sea" who is no longer of concern in* The Master Builder *as is Hilde. Regrettably we must assume for the present perception of matters by the playwright that Ellida had not, as has been assumed previously, achieved "a true marriage." Later, instead, she did in spite of everything go away with "a male stranger." In any case, she did not solve the hovering problems and had not created "a true home," because Hilde, who worshipfully clung to Ellida, says that her home was like "a cage." Therefore, and although she holds her father "so terribly dear," she did not wish to return home, saying, "the bird of the forest will never fly into the cage." And like all of Ibsen's great female figures she is "a bird of the forest," although she differs significantly from them.*

Much critical attention has been devoted to Ibsen's "symbolism" but rarely has it been put into the sharp perspective we find in Lou's general observation: "In all of Ibsen's plays, symbolism plays a role, but mostly it serves only in a truly genial and innovative way to reflect unifyingly in one picture a complicated and deep inner happening alongside an outer event, without either touching the other. Marvelous examples of this mode are seen particularly in *Ghosts* and *The Lady from the Sea.*" The same holds true as well of *Hedda Gabler*.

Lou observes that the accumulation of the gemlike little scenes slowly and precisely trigger the big events. Lou is careful to point to what shaped Hedda before the curtain rises, namely, her social pretensions, sexual stimulations and repression, obeisance to social conventions, flirtations with admirers, and rejection by potential suitors who thought her to be an undesirably capricious and expensive acquisition. All of this knowledge and experience Lou sees as significant in the fixation of Hedda's character traits that dominate her relations with others.

It is true that Ibsen does not have Hedda "discuss herself." That would have been artificial. Hedda rather is the sum total of her actions, gestures, and lines dispersed throughout the play, which offer moments of self-revealment. Lou sees the essence of Hedda's character in her dispirited pose and handling of her father's pistols: "I stand here idly and shoot into the blue sky."

Obviously the pistols are thematically fateful throughout the play. Brilliant in Lou's reading is the perception that Hedda's lack of inner truth and strength causes her to miss all the false targets she has set for herself; only when she sets *herself* up as a target of possible worth does she succeed, "a shot—and nothingness." The emptiness of Hedda's life is caught by her own, dark refrain: "Sometimes it seems as if I have a talent for only one thing in this world . . . to bore myself to death." As Lou comments, Hedda "dies for herself as she had lived for herself."

To Lou, who so consciously used her maiden or married name as it suited her, Ibsen's use of Hedda Gabler rather than Hedda Tesman was striking. Both Lövborg, the would-be lover and companion of Hedda's youth, and Brack, the would-be interloper, wish to nullify or "undo" her marriage by taking advantage of past associations and insisting on calling her Hedda Gabler. Ibsen expressed this in a letter:

> . . . *The title of the play is* Hedda Gabler. *My intention in giving it this name was to indicate that Hedda as a personality is to be regarded rather as her father's daughter than as her husband's wife.*
>
> *It was not really my desire to deal in this play with so-called problems. What I principally wanted to do was to depict human beings, human emotions, and human destinies, upon a groundwork of certain social conditions and principles of the present day.* (From a letter to Count Moritz Prozor, Munich, December 4, 1890)

Up to a reasonable point, Lou's personal identification with certain of Ibsen's female figures can readily be established. But the biographer-critic Binion, for instance, discards caution and takes several leaps into the blue: "Ibsen noted: 'The daemon in Hedda is that she wants to influence another human being, but once that has happened she despises him'. . . . Conceivably Ibsen had heard about Lou to this effect from his friend and noted Danish critic [Georg] Brandes—but without getting her name straight. . . ." Ibsen "also managed to give Hedda Lou's physique by and large and her age [29 years old] as of late 1890, when the play appeared." Ibsen's Hedda, it may be recalled, in the play's text has a face and figure described as "aristocratic and elegant." While Lou was sympathetic to Nora, Hedwig, Ellida, and was "soft" on Rebecca, "Lou was hard as nails on that general's daughter and professor's wife, Hedda Gabler. This mighty animus against Hedda was meant to dissociate Lou from the Lou-like monster wife who would destroy a great work of scholarship in which her husband was involved. . . . Lou on her side produced a work instead [her book on Ibsen's female figures]—and with help from her husband [Andreas]. . . ."

Amid such a mélange of facts, coincidences, and unverifiable conjectures, it is difficult to keep one's bearing. In Binion's animated critique, Lou cannot win: she either identifies with Ibsen's females or dissociates herself from them. Lou could surely not be asked to analyze the personal and emotional motives that prompt her interpretations of Ibsen's figures, but she implicitly measured the experience of Ibsen's female figures relative to the reality of individual and societal conflicts.

Lou's dislike of Hedda owes less to the possible wish to prove herself not to be a "monster wife" and more to Lou's catalogued contempt for Hedda's constant fear of being "compromised" in the eyes of society and the specter of scandal, Hedda's failure to become a purposeful and creative woman, her destructive drives that make a mockery out of creativity, her deceits—nibbling on forbidden fruits—that abort any sensual fulfillment, and her laziness and lack of daring that point to an interior emptiness. Hedda voyeuristically peeks into life instead of participating. Lou expresses admiration for only one of the lines spoken by Hedda. When Counselor Brack, the man without a conscience, unsubtly informs Hedda that he knows Lövborg's death-dealing pistol belongs to Hedda, she fears exposure; but he suavely assures her that there will be no scandal. "No, Hedda Gabler . . . not as long as I keep silent." Hedda then exclaims to the audience: "Unfree. Unfree then! . . . No . . . That thought I cannot endure! Never." To Lou, those "are Hedda's most lovely words . . . though her entire freedom signifies something worthless."

Lou has also caught Ibsen's careful fusion of stage directions, views from windows that allow nature's seasons to have their impact—for nature and persons are paralleled in Ibsen's dramas—and pervasive moods expressed through lighting. With that in mind, Lou explains Ibsen's organic effects: "Hedda is not unripe but rather is like an all-too early decayed autumn." The interior of Hedda is congruent with the baleful autumn that Ibsen fashions as the exterior and enveloping fact of the play. Modern stagings of *Hedda Gabler* perpetuate attention to those elements—psychological and physical—to which Lou had been drawn.

While the list is long of notable Ibsen actresses—from Eleanore Duse to Liv Ullmann, Claire Bloom and Janet Suzman—there were no women critics of Ibsen's plays in the years since Lou Salomé until the contemporary writings of Eva Le Gallienne, Mary McCarthy, Elizabeth Hardwick, and others. Intellectually Lou Salomé is their brilliant precursor, and her revived essays make one aware of her historical role. About women's estimation of themselves and the reflections caught in Ibsen's dramas, there still remain affinities of judgment between Lou and her successors, despite the many decades that separate their writings about Ibsen. That in itself tells us much about the authenticity of Lou's insights and the lasting impact of Ibsen.

I   NORA

> *"After all, it is splendid to be waiting*
> *for a wonderful thing to happen."*

S HORTLY BEFORE CHRISTMAS EVE, a Christmas tree already is in
place in the warm and cozy living room of the newly
appointed bank director Torvald Helmer. Colors shimmer down
from all the tree branches, and the deep, fresh green of the tree
almost disappears amid a glittering shower. In its childish splen-
dor of gilded paper and candles, the tree stands expectantly in the
smile of a waning day, an object not created for sober contempla-
tion. Decorated as handsomely as possible, the tree awaits the fall
of night. In the pomp and glitter, a mysteriously growing light
anticipates twilight, ready to flare up brightly and blindingly, and
to transform everything into a flashing display, into the luminous
miracle of Christmas eve.

Nora's inner life can be reconstructed through the temper
and tone of this impending Christmas eve. Upon her first appearance, she is laden with shrouded holiday parcels; surrounding
her deepest conflicts and dreams are secret festivity and presents.
With a trustful and childlike anticipation of twilight, she awaits a
wonder.

Christmas is a children's festival, and Nora is a child. Her
childishness creates her charm, her danger, and her destiny. As
the sole daughter of a widower who in his carefree ways spoiled
her instead of bringing her up seriously, Nora grew older only in
age. The transformation from her carefree days as a girl to marriage meant no more to her than a change from a small doll's
house to a larger one; the main difference was that instead of her
customary lifeless wax dolls, she would eventually receive three
precious living dolls.

She brought her accustomed love for both play and parent to
her marriage with Helmer; it was a love developed in the relationship between daughter and father—devoted, sincere—in which
she looked upward with the open-eyed adoration of a child.
"When I lived at home," Nora told Doctor Rank, a frequent

visitor, "naturally, I loved father above all else. . . . You can well imagine that being with Torvald is just like being with father."

This childish innocence and inexperience permits her to assume without question that her husband embodies everything that is good and noble, as does a father in the eyes of a child. And so, courtship and marriage must seem to her a superabundant gift which one is obliged to accept thankfully and uncritically; it is also a mysterious and precious gift, toward which one is led blindfolded, with good manners. She is overwhelmed and can hardly grasp the magnitude of the gift, the love offering. For the husband who towers so high above her has not only inclined himself to give fatherly solicitude and accustomed sustenance, but out of his free choice has elevated her to be his wife, to be one with him. It seems to her like an incomprehensible miracle, and she believes in it as a child would. With this sense of the miraculous there awakens in her for the first time a new, exclusive world and a development—a world of humility and pride; an unconstrained giving of herself to her husband; together with the first stirrings of her search for self-identity and worth. The first impulses of her slumbering strength are awakened; instinctively she attempts to come into her own in order to be capable of making a yielding gift of herself. Her slumber is dissipated by anticipatory dreams of a true marriage.

What takes shape in Nora's innermost being temporarily lies hidden from her own sensibility and remains largely unintelligible to her. Within her lies a tender, invisible but prospective seed; that seed is covered by the crisp and proliferating weeds and flowers of her carefree nature. She remains in her small, circumscribed world of play and vanity. High and remote above arches a sky of miracles, and its infinite blue she sees joyously reflected in humans and things. Though distanced from reality, she gradually senses that her relationship with Torvald Helmer is that of a charming child to a parent, and not one of equals. Yet, ever more patiently, she looks for a miracle from above.

"I have waited," she says toward the end, "so patiently for eight years; God knows, I realized quite well that wonderful things cannot come as daily commonplaces." Helmer has no inkling of her expectations. Nothing lies farther from his mind than changing their relationship; in no way does he share Nora's need for self-fulfillment, equality and mutual growth. At the core, she remained childlike, while he was a self-satisfied adult. The wish for growth is a child's pleasure that trustingly demands self-transcendence. For Helmer, that would be as unwelcome as outgrowing accustomed clothes. Considerately, he does not constrain her playful nature, but he must prevent her wish. After all, he had taken her measure and found an undeveloped personality who would fit precisely into that doll's house into which he led her.

Nora's love is at home in some wonderland, while his is anchored in his doll's house. Childlike love entwines itself, like a vine, on the lover, and negligently the toys and dolls of earlier years fall from her hands. The self-satisfied and assured adult, who has no one to look up to, deliberately chooses for his love-object a toy or doll for the idle hours between important business. He chooses a "squirrel" that can perform tricks when he is bored; a "skylark" that can sing away a sour mood; and a "nibbly cat," made sufficiently happy by proffered candy during a light mood. Content with himself and Nora, he smugly says, "I do not want you to be anything but what you are, my lovely, dear little skylark."

It really does not occur to him that it was his love that gave impetus to her development and the extension of her life's horizon, with intimations of something infinite. His sealed doll's house does not lend itself to disruptive change; it must retain his sense of comfortable order. Love in the doll's house cannot be expansive, but can only be added to with gay decorations. Helmer loves the picture of Nora happily humming as she strews the Christmas tree with colorful strips; that, he feels, is her true mission in life. Nothing warns him that the childish birdsong warbling from her lips bridges over into a silent hymn of a blessed—but vain—expectation of a Christmas miracle whose flame can only be lit by him.

Nora does not know that love and beauty have opposite meanings for them both. She does not yet know that Helmer's delight in simple gaiety and loveliness is, at the same time, a conventional person's reluctance to face any serious struggle which could disturb the aesthetic somnolence that allows him to enjoy life with self-satisfaction. It is not without reason then that

Doctor Rank, the sick friend of the family, avoids having Helmer attend to him during his struggle with death. He knows that Helmer has "a pronounced repugnance to anything which is ugly." And not unfittingly is the turn in Nora's destiny entwined with Helmer's in the profound struggle that ensues. The view he offers her turns her love into death.

The apparent moral strength that Helmer fosters, his need to appear above reproach and to retain his dignity without stain, all the self-control evidenced in his daily life, is rooted in a central egotistic pleasure-seeking. On the obverse side, however, there is an unmistakable sign of petty fears—the fears of a human to engage in conflict. The contrast between Nora's naïve judgments, undisciplined inclinations, and inherited disposition to frivolity and lavishness, and Helmer's correct bearing and rectitude most surely intimidate Nora. Appearances are deceiving: his self-satisfaction is disguised by a serious moral mien, while her deep-slumbering seriousness constantly seems to be transformed into a joyful child's face.

Sometimes she is provoked and tosses a lightning expletive into Helmer's nice, tidy, carefully constructed world. And it only takes a stressful situation to produce involuntary quarrels that stem from her actions. Long before their inner differences become evident to her, the seeds of conflict are sown by the many outer dissimilarities between care-free inexperience and well-cultivated strictness.

The possibility of gaining a cure for Helmer—when he was mortally ill—through a prolonged trip south is hampered by lack of money. Nora's pleas that she be allowed to earn money shatter as Helmer forbids her efforts, and her father's death makes it impossible to enlist his help. In desperation she takes a dangerous step. Misled by a lack of experience, she forges her father's name on a bond and cashes a substantial sum; in effect, her borrowing places her in the hands of a pettifogging lawyer (named Krogstad) who pursues a variety of "business deals." Although this was the action of an unknowledgeable child who had always been left in the dark about such matters, Nora, through the years, shouldered the obligatory repayments with the energy and confidence of a man. Pretending that the money is her father's gift, she persuades Helmer to take the necessary vacation. Nora is in deep sorrow over her father's death, fearful for the health of her husband, and about to give birth to her first child. And still she can cajole and wheedle Helmer into believing that he is acceding only to her pleasure-seeking whims; he cannot be permitted to have an inkling of how ill he really is.

Upon Helmer's return home, she does not tell her cured husband of the obligations she has incurred through her action. All alone, secretly, and with tiring work, she undertakes repayment. Under the pretext of wrapping Christmas packages, she sits up nights and does copyist work. Good-naturedly she allows herself to be chided as a "nibbly cat" who wastes the monies for which she has begged, while in fact she had scrimped and skeletonized her own needs so that Helmer and the children had been deprived of nothing. The constant avoidances of the truth come easily to her because of her casual upbringing at home, so that small lies come as readily to her mouth as chirping does to birds. And despite the difficulties of her position, despite her privations, made doubly difficult by her inclinations to be a spendthrift, she feels a unique happiness in her serious and responsible accomplishment.

"It almost seemed to me as if I were a man!" she said. Strength and independence slowly unfold secretly and grope toward release. Although she is left in the dark and enmeshed in a network of lies, there comes the first unconscious expression of protest against her father and husband, both of whom have kept her in bondage to childishness and ignorance. But protest does not surface in her consciousness; on the contrary, she does not wish Helmer to take notice of her awakening self. A fine, feminine instinct decidedly tells her that she must keep the charm she possesses in Helmer's eyes; her naïve love-charms are poised against the sounder, stronger and more intelligent man. It is no dissimulation when she looks up to him with love and admiration. Her childlike façade, that hides much from others, is for Helmer no masking but the visage of true and humble love. With indignation, Nora rejects the advice of her childhood friend, Mrs. Linde, that she confess everything to Helmer, although Nora herself had confided her secret to Mrs. Linde, herself an experienced and diligent person, in order not to appear flighty.

"For heaven's sake, how can you advise that," she answered

Mrs. Linde; "how painful and humiliating would it be for him as a male to know that he owes me something! That would bring our mutual relationship completely out of kilter, and our beautiful, happy homelife will no longer be what it now is!" Despite her hard-won and blissful independence, she does not in the least wish to play her trump card against him and change her admiring glances into the bold ones of an equal partner. It is not the sobriety of a strenuously won equality that she sees in her dreams of a true marriage; she seeks instead the miracle of an incomprehensible love that draws her upward toward him and increases in wonder the higher he, a god, towers over the child. The only value she places on her actions and intrinsic work is that they derive from her love. She excludes any thought that ultimately he could be displeased or indignant at the secret life of her last eight years.

She sums up that life in her confession: "I have loved you above everything in this world!" One cannot work for, nor earn, a miracle. It must surprise one, as does grace, spirituality, poetry. But in nothing do the energetic uniqueness and the urge for completion within her awakening individuality express themselves more clearly than in her recognition that expectation, longing, and trust must willy-nilly be transformed inwardly into creative action. She is not content to let the Christmas mood take its course, but she participates in the pleasure of preparing Christmas gifts. She works at her love-offering for Helmer when she strives to free herself; yet she wants to achieve her freedom only to make him a present of it. In darkness, secrecy, and behind closed doors it originates, destined to be among the Christmas gifts. That makes her proud and happy, expectant of a transformation.

The appearance of her old friend, Mrs. Linde, casts a harsh and sober pall over Nora's festive joy; Mrs. Linde resembles the hard workday—cold, joyless, and as grubby as her relentless work for bare necessities. The prohibition of every outer luxury, of everything that could be done without, constricted and oppressed Mrs. Linde's inner life; the potential richness of her nature was emasculated, and only utilitarian and sensible considerations found expression. Long ago she turned her back on the practicing lawyer Krogstad, a man she loved, and contracted a marriage that made the financial support of her mother, sisters, and brothers possible. And after a sad and bleak marriage, her husband died and left her nothing—not even a child to care for. Now she offers Krogstad her hand in order to save him from the shipwreck of his existence. From her bitterness and loneliness she gathers whatever resources her heart once possessed, and she seeks one last, modest luxury within the long, tiring work-days of her life: *not* to work only and alone for one's bare necessities. Nora, on the contrary, draws this culminating conclusion from her marriage: "I have responsibilities to myself alone." That precisely was the most burdensome of all responsibilities for Mrs. Linde, and from which she now wishes to free herself at all cost. Nora later directs her gravest reproach against her husband's sealing her off from life, seriousness and experience, while Mrs. Linde, amid her coarse and lonely wanderings, searches for only one thing—a last, though modest, refuge from the battles of existence, which would house her love and care. It is like the fir-tree standing alone and forgotten in the wintry woods, prey to storms, not dreaming of Christmas lights and wonders; it knows what it is like to freeze outdoors and wishes to be used up in service to others, to bring warmth and happiness and comfort into peaceful homes, even if it means being the warmth-bringing comfort of a fired stove and not the aura of a Christmas celebration.

At the moment that Mrs. Linde sees her old friend, Krogstad, he is about to use Nora's forgery of her father's signature on the bond as blackmail against Helmer who has dismissed him from his minor clerical post at the bank. Only desperation drives Krogstad to such a step; for the sake of his motherless children, he must retain his hard-won place in society. He himself was out-lawed by society for similar forgeries in his devious business dealings. Mrs. Linde's determination to marry him and be a mother to his children has an ennobling, mellowing effect upon him. The unexpected gift of trust and friendship awakens his good qualities, whereas his former friend, Helmer, in a short time will prove himself to be a selfish coward with regard to Nora's great love and trust. Helmer is a weakling whose only concern is with his reputation in society. In Krogstad's happy desire to again be worthy of his lover, he stands as high over Helmer as does

Mrs. Linde over Nora, in respect to patience, experienced goodness, and maturity. And so, Mrs. Linde's words, "we need each
other," initiate the life of a true marriage, despite struggles with
inevitable problems, while Nora's dream about her marriage and
belief in the integrity of her husband collapse.

Krogstad's threat to tell Nora's husband everything and to
note that the bank director's wife is guilty of the same type of
forgery that he himself had committed earlier, makes Nora aware
for the first time of her endangered position. She now realizes
that she is a guilty party in the eyes of the law. But she is even
more disturbed when she hears from Helmer about the aversion
inspired in him by a man like Krogstad who has committed a
misstep without atoning for it; how such a person creates a
corrupt environment, and how he spins a web of lies in which his
children must grow up. Nora's fears rise and her well-kept secret
no longer is a source of pride but an oppressive burden on her
conscience. She makes every effort to persuade Helmer to rehire
Krogstad. In vain. But at the same time that her adamant husband
turns away her request he involuntarily affords an insight into the
motives that make him so inflexible. Strangely affected and sur-
prised, she sees that the main reasons for his attitude need not be
sought in moralistic indignation. After all, he admits that he
could have "overlooked perhaps" Krogstad's mistake. But "what
if it were to become known that 'the new bank director's wife
changed his mind for him'?"

And as for Guenther Krogstad, he was the reminder of an
old, unfortunate friendship, and "of this that tactless person
makes no secret. . . . I assure you that this is most painful for
me." Nora can hardly believe her ears; "Torvald, you can't be
serious. . . . No, these are only trifles."

Here is her first, astonished insight into Helmer's basic character, piercing deep through the cloud of smug satisfaction in
which he hovers above her. But danger and fear hem her in, so
that her first feeling of strangeness regarding Helmer does not yet
become a conscious estrangement. She does make a last,
strenuous effort to save herself; she will ask Doctor Rank, and
hopes to be able to placate Krogstad.

Yet her twilight conversation with the sick family-friend elicits a confession that voids her plan. In that dialogue, a well-

rounded Nora emerges: she is indiscreet and childish, yet at the
same time exhibits fine tact and the instinct of a mature woman—
frivolous, capable of lying and coquetry, and yet there is purity
clear to the roots of her being. She is inexperienced but has a
noble and inherent disposition for the fullest self-education. With
that last, shattered attempt, her hesitation and vacillations end;
she becomes resolute. To Mrs. Linde she says, "You must prevent nothing." She knows that she is approaching a point of
crisis: Helmer will find out everything and she will be lost. But
she also knows that something else must occur at the same
time—the wonderful thing, the revelation of his love which will
intercede for her and take everything upon itself; a love that will
cast her not as a playful and charming child but as a wife who has
sacrificed herself for Helmer, who now will sacrifice himself for
her.

Night descends and the glow and glitter of the day fades;
with the first approach of darkness, the beaming Christmas wonder also draws near. To doubt it would also be to doubt Helmer's
magnanimity and the greatness of his love. What may be punish-
able in the light of uncomprehending and unreasonable human
laws, must instead be recognized by Helmer as the proof of her
love; what appear to the judgment of strangers to be lies and
deception will undoubtedly be regarded by Helmer as the blessed
secret of a child who worked in stolen moments on Christmas
gifts, and who then impatiently awaits her own.

She would not, however, accept his sacrifice; she would not
want him to suffer for her sake. She will want to bear fully the
consequences of her actions, to crawl silently out of his life, and
through her death validate his innocence in all that happened.
Even the thought of her children does not deter her from such
intentions; it is painfully consoling to know that the children will
find a better mother in her old and devoted governess. She has
not as yet identified herself with the role of mother, nor indeed
that of wife. Like a bride, instead, she remains in expectation of a
true marriage. Only then would her own life be crowned and
fulfilled, and she would learn of her exclusive mission.

For these reasons—and at that moment—she is able to subdue her thoughts about Helmer and the children. Heroically she
is able to turn away from them, believing herself about to see the

full unfolding of a wonder, like a child who peeks through door-cracks and spies the bustle about the Christmas tree and the first sparkle of lights. Despite all the fears, dangers, and sacrifices that mark the most important and deadly struggle in her life, a confession wells up: "After all, it is splendid to be waiting for a wonderful thing to happen." It is not to be. Nevertheless, for her to find such words speaks of her power, and lays claim to an audacious idealism from which rise, at the end, all her harshly true, sacred and measured words.

In stark contrast to her powerful mood, she is busy preparing for a masked ball, as the fateful letter from Krogstad is dropped into the mailbox of the house. While rehearsing steps for her dance, a *tarantella*—she tries to distract Helmer's attention from the letter.

In her efforts to seem unconcerned, Nora's usual frivolity bursts into abandoned and feverish wildness. What has matured and moved her far beyond the childish and the playful, she can only hide behind a mask in painful costuming. And so, her married life with Helmer expresses itself in an an impromptu near manic performance of a studied dance, which he watches with harmless pleasure. Nothing warns him that this display of charm, this ultimate childlikeness, represents precisely the mere appearance of a boundless love, costumed for him yet one more time on her deathlike journey—while secretly she has readied a sober dress for a long wandering.

Helmer sees only the attractiveness of this love which lies intoxicatingly over her silent farewell. Champagne has roused his senses and stimulated desire for his wife. The words with which he pictures his intoxication are the replete expression of the poetry that streams from Nora to him, as well as of the worthlessness of his character which cannot cull anything deeper from such a love than a captive ornament for his comfortable existence. Delirium and love therefore dissipate as rapidly as does the champagne's inebriation. The letter lies in his hands. With tortured fright he is seized by the fear of the consequences of Nora's past actions on his behalf. In manic anger, he heaps scorn upon Nora and casts her out from his heart—but not from his home, because he wishes to keep appearances up for the sake of outsiders.

For Nora, things collapse; she feels as if the world were suddenly godless. Silent and petrified she stands before Helmer. What had remained to be taught her of cares and experience, now is completed in one instant: she suddenly sees life as it is, in the shape of Helmer, a conventional, pained person who is saturated with fear and selfishness. All her life and attentiveness has been focused on him. Since her life was sustained by *his* truth and interpretations, only through *him* could her life be shorn of God and thus destroyed. Even if her maturity had grown equal to the experience of this hour, her childlike heart in its depth retained faith, and her life its wonders. Even if everything else—independence and personal growth—lay waiting in anticipation, this new and singular situation launched her emancipation.

And in the midst of Helmer's outbreaks of fear and anger comes Krogstad's second letter, accompanied with the bond, written in the mellow mood of his new-found happiness. "I am saved!" is Helmer's first outcry, "Nora, I am saved." Quietly she asks, "And I?" Obviously, she too is saved. And now, in a new light, she is clear about her situation and their relationship. With one blow, her moral indignation evaporates. Helmer sympathetically acknowledges her struggles and assures Nora of his willingness to forgive her. Indeed, he finds her doubly touching in her inexperience and helplessness; he assures Nora that her weakness endears her to him all the more because he can serve now as her strength and support to protect and guide her.

To Nora, it seems that she had been reduced to a lapdog which was whipped and then restored to grace, or that she had been treated like a doll which one discards and then picks up at the dictate of whim. With terrible and blinding clarity she becomes conscious of the fact that she had been a life-long toy and that she had lost her dignity in accommodating herself to others. Something strange and immeasurable changes her make-up. Her slowly awakening strength and independence—everything she had so humbly and busily gathered together for the gift of love she was going to bestow from her integral inner humanity—now rears up and wrests itself free in enormous protest. And so, a new, strange, strong human being is born, no longer kneeling nor enslaved nor able to be deceived.

And what has silently and overwhelmingly developed now

finds expression. Awakened and without chains, Nora stands before Helmer and declares her freedom, simply, clearly, unconstrainedly. To the objections of an experienced and cautious mind, she seems naïve and still childish, but her unimpeachable, forward-looking, magnificent naïveté penetrates to the heart of things.

Helmer senses that they are dealing with elementals. And his objections and reproaches slowly yield to deep astonishment at the Nora who faces him. To him she is a strange and incomprehensible figure, without any resemblance to his little, childish Nora of the past. She is an oppressive and terrible enigma, and his only possible solution is expressed in the outcry, "So, only one explanation is possible: You don't love me anymore!"

No, she does not love him any longer. Actually, she had never loved him, only another, a completely different person. He is a stranger under whose roof she can no longer remain. She was never happy under his roof, "only merry." And now, when she looks back, it seems to her as if she had lived like a poor person "from hand to mouth." She had been impoverished. As for her real inner life, she had to give it in secret installments amid stolen moments and untruths. How could anyone dare assume jurisdiction over her inner life before she herself came into her own? How could one dare to hand her over to someone else before she was capable of giving herself? How could it be permitted that she became a mother who gave birth to children before she gave birth to a personality within her freed from the constriction of the childish? Or before two humans had matured, how could she know that they were growing toward a compatible goal? How could she know if they would fuse in mind and spirit? Or if within their reach was that rare, crowning and human apex: "a true marriage?"

Nora is not able to experience love and marriage in Mrs. Linde's way—full of rationality, habituation, renunciation and sober duty—a love and marriage without the element of wonder. That which had been robbed from the life of the "inner" Mrs. Linde existed with idealistic and abundant measure in Nora. Earlier, she had not really known if ideals were the elements which filled her depths. Ideals live inseparable from play and dreams, like happy siblings or children who consort with angels.

A child casually assumes that a guardian angel watches from above and protects one from stumbling, from disturbances in sleep. But then, human fate enters: no guardian angel protects one's steps on the journey with its pitfalls, nor prevents a hateful awakening to a sober, everyday, gross reality. For the first time, ideals and reality are split by a gaping chasm. And for the first time, the die is cast: are her dreams and hopes only the imaginings of a child or the battle-ready and fairytale hulls of ideals ready to cope with life? Once upon a time, everything was based on trust, free from worry or care; now everything stands in doubt. Once upon a time, the wondrous was taken for granted; now everything—even the most obvious and certain—that had been taught her appears gnarled and incomprehensible.

In such a moment, a child helplessly gropes for the hand of the adult in order to find guidance and direction; but another type of childlikeness, intimately related to the ideals of life, can rapidly gather strength and masculine force. Far from subduing Nora or attuning her to compromise, the first decisive conflict acts upon her like a battle cry. . . . Resistance and bravery harden into armor. She has grasped that the peaks of wonder in life do not appear as readily as fairies who awaken Sleeping Beauty; in life, peaks must be conquered. That insight she is willing to put to the test. . . .

And so, we leave Nora at the entrance into the unknown vastness of life, which opens darkly. Nothing as yet tells her if she will find a way toward her goal. No longer is the blue, arched sky comforting and enveloping. It is far and remote, and separated seemingly by immeasurable distances from the ground upon which she stands lost. Far, far at the horizon's outermost bleakness, there is a thin line wherein heaven and earth flow together within the ken of the human eye, promising reconciliation. With every step toward the horizon's line, what seems ideal recedes, and yet one journeys into the endless.

Despite such premonitions, a calm and dominating force within her courage and faith impels her to overcome Helmer. The masculinity and conscientiousness of her childlike persistence render Helmer's weapons—experience and insight—useless. In the midst of his self-awareness and contentment, he strangely senses a secret power to which he must bow. Helmer, who had looked down upon Nora with considerate condescension, finds himself responding humbly to the determination of her childlike idealism, with this promise: "I have the strength to become someone else."

It seems to him as if the child in him had awakened from a deep sleep, a child which can still grow. . . . Only slowly does this sense rise. Not as with the determined, joyous strength of Nora but tearfully, hesitantly, helplessly; his soul—confused, unsure—in darkling pain searches for its lost childhood. For that reason, he possesses no strength to bind Nora to himself. He has no choice but to listen to the door as it falls into its lock as Nora leaves. Yet he does not turn from her without hope. He sits, staring wide-eyed after her, hunched into himself, silent.

For the first time, everything which until now has filled him with daily worries and joys—his old world—slowly sinks. For the first time, all her tumult and busy alarms are petrified into a deep, soundless silence; and slowly, slowly, with a dreamlike magic, Nora's world reappears. From all the corners and crevices of the abandoned room, out of its quite cold isolation, it seems as if old, forgotten fairytales gather around him like ghostly, childish figures at play. He had lived with all those figures for so long during his marriage without seeing in them anything more profound than toys and objects of delight, and without noticing the pinions on their small shoulders capable of lifting him out of *his* narrow doll house.

II MRS. ALVING

"Now I see what happened. . . . And now I can speak out.
And yet, no ideals will collapse."

I F THE UNATTAINABLE and the uncertain is implied by the idea of "wondrous," it also contains unlimited possibilities and perspectives. If it is a battle and no victory that Nora is about to encounter, she is ready with a youthful, strong, and golden armor. If she parts in pain, it is not mere sorrowful and patient acceptance of a pain that comes from the loss of ideals but a contention and striving for a new ideal. She is imbued with refreshing boldness which bodes promise and beginning—the ending remains open. She only crosses the threshold where life—the chosen path of life—first begins. For that reason the drama of her development and her protest against every suppression of her growth are only the prelude to the tragedy that engulfs her successor—Helene Alving.

Like Nora, Helene steps from a limiting girlhood and immaturity into marriage. But instead of a gay doll house, she finds herself growing up in a school of rigid habits and religious indoctrination, and instead of titillating play that robs Nora of seriousness and truth, dreary demands of responsibility act as bars to her unfolding as a personality in the freedom and joy of authentic life.

These impressions during adolescence explain why Helene's first, innocent enthusiasm is directed to a clergyman; she needs a minister in order to fuse her dark, life-yearning drive with his studied, earnest discipline. Yet it appears equally and emphatically significant that this Pastor Manders is a naïve idealist, replete with harmless pretensions and untainted spirituality, upon whom she bestows the first, free stirrings of her heart. This sheds a touching light on the transition from girlhood to the tragedy of a marriage through which she is victimized by coarseness and degradation.

The shy dream of her first love has no power to protect her from the tragedies ahead. It is the same reverence for what is held sacred and pure, represented by Pastor Manders, that impels Helene in her choice of a husband and presses her to bow to the God-willed authority of her family. And so, she agrees to marry the young, wealthy army officer Alving, who is considered a "good catch," despite his loose living that is in such marked contrast to the austerity of his environment.

Wherever Alving appeared, "it was like Spring weather. And then, his tireless strength and liveliness. . . . And now, this hedonistic child, for at that time he acted like one, had to wander around a middle-sized city that could offer only pleasantries rather than heady pleasures. Here he had to stay in a minor occupation, without purpose in life. He saw no prospects for work which would engage his energies. He had no friend who could share the joy of life; he had only drinking companions and consorted only with idlers."

Perhaps he dreamed of a wife and house, a lovely homestead to satisfy his needs. And perhaps the contentment and beauty of such living would have stirred her like the pealing of a pure bell. But Helene could not have known this. She says of herself, "I was taught something about duties and the like, in which I had believed until the present; everything terminates in duties, mine and his."

Despite her obedient consent, Helene does not face her husband with Nora's childlike naïveté. One thing has fully developed within the limitations of her dogmatic upbringing, namely, the inner compulsion to judge everything strictly from the standpoint of the ideal and the religious. She is far from seeing, as Nora did, that marriage is a blessed and humbly received gift. Helene sees in marriage a challenge for herself and her husband. As a girl with an unripe mind, she is unable to assess and understand things correctly. And yet, she judges him instantly by comparing him with a preconceived idealized picture against which, in any case, his natural youthful strength must appear coarse and dissolute. Instead of freely drawing from his vitality and releasing herself from a bleak upbringing, she raises a barrier between them from the start, with all the acquired strength and coldness of her own schooling.

From the start, her husband becomes estranged and disappointed; then rejected, he flees the house and takes up again the pleasures and distractions of his earlier days. To the same degree that Helene's indignation and contempt rise, he sinks deeper and deeper in the choice of his pleasures, until after a year of marriage she is justified in calling him an absolute libertine.

A wild and overwhelming disgust seizes her, which breaks through all the preconceptions and schooling she had brought into the marriage. She takes refuge with the spiritual friend of her home, Pastor Manders. Although the tender effusion of her dreamlike girlishness prevents self-assertion, there occurs the first unconscious expression of her indignant nature, a sudden and abrupt outcry, a cry she takes up instantaneously and ruthlessly. She had permitted the marriage knot to be tied because she had been taught to believe in the sacramental union of marriage; stronger, however, than obedience is her dark inner sense that justifies the tearing of a knot which she recognizes to be neither unifying nor sacramental.

In the passionate power of this awareness, her enthusiasm for a man of purity, who is the object of her childlike imaginings, gains heightened importance: he must appear to her almost as the incarnation of all her strict and sensitive ideals; moreover, the effective desacralising of her ideals drives Helene away from her husband. Only in this sense is it possible for her to come to her friend Manders, with the cry, "I am here. Take me!"

This cry does not wrest itself from an irresponsible woman but from a horrified child whose eyes are opened to the hateful and gross in life; it is no demand for the delights of love but a flight from her defilement. All the injured and angered stirrings of her nature burst into a passionate self-offering that stems from inner purity and innocence.

During the course of her later life, for that reason, the personal impulse that drove her to Manders, and that initially gave her the strength to break with accustomed obedience, becomes increasingly pronounced until it dominates and changes her existence: she is determined to shake off what she has perceived as untruth and to pursue and bow only to truth.

The wild arousal of her nature could have, indeed, meant her emancipation if only the husband toward whom her admiration and trust had been directed were not the eager representative of all the ossified and disciplined doctrines of her own upbringing.

Distraught and displeased with the sacrilege of her flight, Manders resists every offered temptation and directs her return, as a matter of duty, to her husband, however dissolute he may be. She is obliged to maintain the marriage, sealed before God, and devote herself to it in the future as the only goal and ideal.

As yet, her personality has not developed sufficiently to decline obedience to tradition; once again, she bows to it. What she had pursued half-thinkingly in a passive acquiescence grounded in her education, she now consciously fashions into the content and goal of her life. She shuns no struggle nor sacrifice to set obstacles in the path of her husband's philanderings; these obstacles remain useless because they can serve only the same rigid measures that had driven him away from her into isolation. She cannot now heal his pleasure-seeking because earlier she had neither understood nor entered into it. And so, despite every struggle for a true marriage, she is unable to merge seriousness and the joy of life, moodiness and frivolity; she can only preserve the outer appearance of marriage. So that no one may perceive the sad secret within her marriage and know of her husband's life, she keeps him securely in her home by yielding to his voluptuary tastes; she offers herself as partner to his despicable orgies, drinks and laughs with him until she is sure of his secure tranquillity. As with her body, she cloaks the sacrament of her marriage from external view.

Even this remains without success because her husband pursues intimate relations with the domestic maid, a relationship that has fateful consequences. From that point on, Helene determinedly wrests from him both his authority and freedom. She becomes as much his tyrant as earlier she had been his near-whore. And while he slowly and passively sickens under the impact of a disease incurred by corruption, she takes firm measures to put all suspicions to rest by linking his name and resources to charitable enterprises, preserving his name and reputation. Thanks to her resoluteness, he was held in esteem as a gentleman up to the time of his death. Her self-imposed task is bolstered by her concern for her only child, Oswald, who represented her sole source of happiness. And yet, she sent him abroad for his education so that he would not breathe the poisoned atmosphere of the home; when he returns home after his father's death, he would at least retain untainted ideals.

That is the external appearance of her life's course: the pursuit of a traditional goal, without inner conflicts or doubts. But her adaptation to conventions was not without struggle, and this lonely and desperate struggle eventually developed her total energies and independence. In this respect, her personality is steeled and it breaks the bondage of submission to piety. It becomes clear to her that the goals for which she continues to battle, and for which she had suffered, had been imposed from without and that they do not stem from her own convictions.

The idealized motto inscribed over the entrance to her life was not written by her; she was under the devotional delusion that a divine hand had indelibly inscribed it in gold. Her first instinctive decision was different; it was spontaneous rejection and flight. Then she had to develop according to imposed criteria and to battle for what she neither stood for nor wanted. And so it was that her actions belonged to her inherited conventions, while their implications put her in doubt. With every victory over herself, she clearly realized the tragic subversion of her own interests and disposition. With that, her first instinctive flight from imposed duty culminates slowly and terribly in a tragic division of her inner life; after sacrifice and victimization, she finally realizes that she has fought a false war and that the gods under whose banner she had fought were ghosts and disembodied shadow-pictures.

In this battle and dividedness, her inner being is in turmoil, so that she could not raise against her own marriage Nora's reproach that marriage had kept her as tightly closed as an unripe bud. Forcefully and ruthlessly Helene's buds are torn open, not by the natural light rays of the sun, but through the disgusting influence of a repulsive and unnerving power that resembles a crawling, devouring worm which opens up buds only to defoliate them.

If, however, she must in this fashion buy knowledge with a leaf from her blossoming life, she must also take the detour that marks a mutilated and sacrificed—instead of a naturally unfolding—life, in order to reach the truth: for all that, one must reach it!

Her deepest instincts tell her that this is both possible and necessary, despite everything. The cast of her mind justifies completely and retrospectively the passionate outcry with which she hurled herself into the arms of Manders, who personified in her childish eyes the true and the pure. It is the same cry that wrenches loose from her after pain and struggle when she faces the most painful import of the truth. Like a battle-weary hero in an untenable position, with no lament, she had seen everything around her decimated, one thing after another, without retreating in defeat. Then on the eve of battle, she sinks to her knees, overwhelmed by shame and longing, with words that declare her youth humbly and honestly: "I am here. Take me!"

For Pastor Manders her cry, at any rate, retains, even in the light of truth, the same frivolous, sinful meaning as it previously had—as he himself was judged by it. When he visits Mrs. Alving after Oswald's return to his mother and for the first time learns about the latter course of her marriage, he is quite naturally upset, but he is also indignant about the turn of her attitudes. And precisely as in the years earlier, he only has this reaction: ". . . and what will become of ideals?"

And in her reply also, grounded in painfully matured clarity, is that which once moved her in passion and confusion, as she simply poses a counterquestion: "And what about the truth?"

Without a trace, life has passed the goodhearted and goodnatured Pastor Manders by. Life had revealed nothing to him, and in his guilelessness and naïveté, there exists neither untruth nor impurity—no matter how obvious their presence. It is easy for him to be deceived and exploited. Mrs. Alving soon is witness to that when the carpenter Engstrand, lame in body and mind, pulls the wool over Manders' eyes; nevertheless, the Pastor, proud of his knowledge of humans, triumphantly exclaims, "What do you say now, Mrs. Alving?"

What does she say? She allows him his triumph. And as she approaches him, her soul is diffused with an indescribably deep grace toward Manders whose advice and persuasion led to the destruction of her fortunes: "I do believe, Pastor Manders, that you are a big infant, and will ever be one!—And, I also think that it would give me pleasure to put my arms around your neck."

Lovely words! And doubly nice because in them is expressed the contrast between her mature control and the conquered, old ideals of youth. From the vantage point of her lonely, steep, and

62   MRS. ALVING

stony heights she looks down—but, with warmth, compassion, and nostalgia, as a strong and tested man looks down upon a beloved child one has outgrown. No recrimination, and no ridicule, no sharpness or bitterness—not even one accusation; nothing except a silent gazing that transcends by far everything personal. There is something grand in her prim bearing with which she manages her suffering and fate. It is the superlative trait of her expansive womanly nature to gather all personal agony and experience into silent understanding and perception.

This trait is nothing more than her longing for truth, which emanates from all the confusion and the striving to shape her own personality. This longing pushes her life into a tragic direction, divided by action directed against her own longings; she converted pain into perception and lament into generosity.

Her earliest actions had set a decisive course, and therefore she could not be saved from the ensuing tragic events. Her ultimate, human delusion is the belief that she can escape the consequences of her past, with the burial of her husband, and could be able to chart a new life with Oswald. For once, there is happiness in such delusion. She is happy to be able to love, with all her accumulated and suppressed tenderness, another being, and to bring unreserved mother love and sacrifice to bear, instead of being sacrificed to the demands of despised duties. And as part of this new and great happiness, she makes one concession to her duties inherited from the past, an honoring that does no honor to truth, namely, the retention of reverence for the image of the father in the son's memory, a final and gentle prevention of hurt for the dead as well as the living.

And Oswald seems to justify the unbounded pride of this mother; in alien surroundings, he had grown beautiful and industrious as a talented painter. All his paintings breathed sunshine and a passion for life, all "centered on a joyousness of life."

In that manner, the philandering pleasure-seeking of his father had become transformed in Oswald into the artistic sense; it was as if the spiritual inheritance from his mother contributed something dignified and silent to the transformation. But that mother's blessing could not eradicate the curse of the father which lay upon Oswald. In the monotonous village and home-life, and with a despondency fostered by the grayness of the rains that hindered his out-of doors pleasures, Oswald begins to favor wine and an intimacy with the domestic maid Regina. He has not the slightest suspicion that she, the daughter of a previous maid, is his half-sister. But Mrs. Alving sees arising from all this the first ghost out of the past; others will soon follow rapidly and inexorably.

Tearfully Oswald confesses that the cause of his alleged travel weariness lies in some malady of the brain that had already led to a spell of madness. His fear of its recurrence had brought him back home; the doctor's diagnosis pointed to his eventual decline into incurable idiocy. Bitter self-reproaches merged with his deadly terror; he feared that he himself had incurred the terrible malady through what seemed to be simple, youthful diversions, and he indignantly brushed away the doctor's surmises that the cause could be found in the philandering life of his father. With Oswald's confession, Mrs. Alving's hope about being able to free herself from the past collapses. At the same time, the inferno that engulfs the orphanage built in the memory of her husband is like the fire that sweeps into her life, and with one cascading glow levels everything to the ground in ashes.

Yet even here the deep drive, which has triggered her tragic experiences and pains, does not disavow its aim to recognize and heed the call of truth. Along with her last happiness sinks her last veil. Not only does a conflagration scorch and destroy; it throws a wide circle of brilliant light around itself and high into the sky. And so, the red-glowing flame that with finality destroyed her life's happiness also brings her clear revelations and illuminations.

It is through Oswald that she is consumed. He complains that he has fled back to their home because of fear, but that now the melancholy monotony of their home overwhelms him with dismal thoughts. And the gray cloud of melancholy and depression, like the rain cloud outside that obliterates everything sunny, awakens an involuntary propensity for indecent and forbidden pleasures, and brings a harvest of perverse desires out of youthful yearnings that had lain fallow.

Mrs. Alving listens to him silently, and in her inner vision, the past unfolds in a new light. It seems to her as if her husband had reappeared as she had known him in his first youthful and unquenchable vitality; it seems to her as if he points to Oswald as his advocate. Is it not, above all, the brooding atmosphere at home and the lack of activity and joyousness which drives Oswald into his father's tracks? Would he not have to become what his father was? It becomes clear to her that what Oswald never tires of glorifying in his sunlit, joy-breathing paintings is merely the artistic expression of the same longing that impelled his father to look for the sun in a life darkened by an overcast sky.

At the same time that the tragedy of her past fulfills itself through Oswald and mercilessly repeats itself like a returning ghost, the tragedy reveals itself in all its causative dimensions. And therefore, the tragedy becomes transformed in him. That ghost no longer appears in Mrs. Alving's eyes like a despised and discarded figure which awakens shudders and disgust; it blossoms in Oswald's youthful beauty and drives, not with a lecherous and coarse outlook, but with ardent pining. The ugliest truth has been removed from Mrs. Alving, like a repugnant burden that has weighted her down. Her judgment of the past is no longer condemnatory; it is only an immeasurable lament and commiseration. She is able to forgive, without disturbing the truth, because she is able to understand.

And with it, she gains courage to deal truthfully with Oswald by taking away his self-reproaches when she shows him what his father was really like. She does this with almost delighted confidence, despite Pastor Manders' indignation at her declaration: "Now I see what happened! And now I can speak out! . . . And yet, no ideals will collapse!"

In that declaration rejoicingly rings the possibility of a reconciliation of the split in her life. What the enforced upholding of the sacrament of tradition was unable to accomplish, was achieved by an objective realization: she was not able to match lovingly the spirit and essence of her husband, nor to open her gentle soul to him. Up until now, the truth had mercilessly stalked her life and had destroyed her ideals, but she pursued it unafraid with passionate intensity. Now the truth with its all-encompassing glow finally enveloped her, so that she could now view and revere the ideal and the truth as a new and triumphant unity.

In this brief scene, the drama peaks, completing its inner

development. It is like the aftermath of the burning orphanage; the glow of the subsiding conflagration drives ghostly clouds of smoke against a dark evening sky. And yet, the glare of the destruction has turned into a soft glow that hovers over Mrs. Alving as she bravely attends to her stricken and tortured child. And in the softness of his illuminating glow, her totally destroyed life stands in noble transformation—tragic though conciliated.

What then follows is the last, inevitable course of outer fate: Oswald's outbreak of madness and Mrs. Alving's oath that she will give him the liberating poison. She will give it to him, she will do it with a symbolic gesture: she will be compelled to destroy with her own hand what she has built up on a false foundation, just as she had to disavow and recant what she had bred and defended in her involuntary mistakes.

With the poison in her hesitating hand, hunched over Oswald during this last night, she struggles through her last earthly battle amid total isolation, in the overwhelming anguish of a mother. And the day breaks above the mountains. Ghostly veils still rest in the depths, and ghostly shadow pictures rise from the valleys. Above them at the highest peak, the quivering, purplish morning is revealed to the eye.

That vision floats before Oswald's dusky consciousness and the inhabitants of the valley—like a dream vision of happiness and blessing which he longingly and dreamily greets with a stammer, "The sun!" Mrs. Alving's clear vision sees things differently. She knows that she must remain until the last in the depths and under the shadows, never to scale those sunny heights; yet, the sun will rise for her and she will be granted a flash of clarity—and with it her release.

For Mrs. Alving, the perceived ideal no longer is the same as that for which Nora, who was ready for the struggle with youthful confidence, searched: a future wondrous happening that lay hidden beyond the distant horizon. For Mrs. Alving, there is no future, no line of the horizon where heaven and earth seem to merge harmoniously; she can only cast a glance upward and backwards upon an abandoned battlefield, strewn with the sacrifices that marked her life. Instead of Nora's wobbling search for insight and development, instead of her painful, first parting from accepted and beloved ideals, Helene Alving has already been immersed in the truth, has experienced it, and has grasped it with capable and firm hands. And so, in place of Nora's hopeful and contentious battle for ideals and truth, tranquillity and peace come to Helene Alving. She does not, like Nora, wander into the unforeseeable, dark distance; she may rest quietly under a sky which has been illuminated. She lifts her face and hands toward the great transformation that breaks into her life, toward the truth—toward the sun.

III HEDWIG

"And she . . . died for the love of me."
—Hjalmar

I F WE PROCEED from the peak of understanding reached by Mrs. Alving, from the peace achieved in her liberation by truth, then it seems that only one thing could impel a return to the ferment and the unrest of life, and that would be the impulse of a selfless mission to bring the blessing and the releasing clarity of knowledge to others.

The representative of such a mission would not appear in the guise of a Nora who favors the ideal right to her own development; he would have to be an apostolic figure who discards his own life, who preaches and exhorts in the midst of the erring, groping masses.

Instead of the lonely figure and the solitary fate that dominate Ibsen's *A Doll's House* and *Ghosts,* we see in *The Wild Duck* a circle of people grouped around an intellectual midpoint that focuses on "the claim of the ideal."

Gregers, the representative of that "claim" and the carrier of that ideal mission, seems to have in fact descended from that airy peak to which Mrs. Alving had aspired. It is as if on those heights her mute and prayerful thoughts were made flesh; while Gregers descends from the heights of pure ideality into real life. If he had made an end to his own strivings and personal hopes, he did so unlike Mrs. Alving whose anguished maturity came with devastating conflicts and a long and trying life. The influences that early led to his disinclination for achievement and drove him into solitude were absorbed passively from the life of his parents. . . .

In the isolated wooded mountains were his father's mining works. There he grew up with a naïve expansiveness, and with the childish belief in an ideal mission to which people would be receptive. With a full heart he descends to them like one who is joyously conscious of bringing something precious and who can lavish his idealistic riches upon anyone in need. He comes to rejoice, to enlighten, to bless like a cheerful emissary from the true home of the spirit. Yet, he is unaware that his ideals are too harsh and burdensome and could have as brooding and imposing an effect as mighty heavenward-rearing mountains set in the midst of a flat plain. So he stands like an almost childish figure amid the puzzled commoners, and this tremendous contrast never permits him to gain firm footing on the earth nor—despite a strong and penetrating will—to achieve successful action. We always see him with outspread or clasped hands, in blessing or admonition; never do they serve to shape matters creatively; never do they clench into compelling fists relative to life. His brutal authoritarian assaults therefore claim victory over him; his mission to free through the truth appears tragic.

An interesting parallel may be drawn between Gregers and the like-minded idealist Brand (in Ibsen's drama of the same name written during his youth). Indisputable is the deep strain of their relation; both are embodiments of "the claim of the ideal" in its total severity and naïveté, without equivocation or restraint, hesitation or doubt. Only the manner in which their intellect develops into action is different. Unlike Gregers, Brand possesses the compelling power symbolic of the fist; he knows how to bend the world to his will. The inflexibility of the material with which he wrestles makes him all the harder—not unsure—and his hardness brings results. Even though Brand ends in failure, it is not because he has failed to accomplish what was humanly possible, but because what he has aimed for, due to the false conception of his ideal, has not taken into account human limitations. Defeat lies in the tragically Faustian figure that is arrested on the borders of human activity and human perceptions. At the same time that the heavens open over the dying Brand and a voice filled with divine mercy speaks to him, it becomes a lived experience of such compassion that it also resembles a judgment pronounced upon his life. Just as the portrait of a youth differs from that of an adult, so Gregers' portrait distances itself from Brand's. Gregers is not hard and merciless like Brand; but he also does not exert any force over life. Just as Brand errs in his conception of God, so Gregers erred in his conception of people—both making it impossible for their ideals to gain fulfillment. For that reason, an inconsolable concern for the nobility of mankind and its deviations also overwhelms him. From above (no less punishingly than above Brand) is heard the divine voice: "He is *Deus caritatis!*" . . . the God of love.

Representing the belief in the brutal powers of life—which defeat Gregers—is the physician Relling. It is noteworthy that he does not appear as a wordmonger of an ideal-impoverished everyday life, but as a surrogate for the ideal. He admits that man is special and that he often needs more than naked reality can offer in order to endure it. He also admits that, for this reason, ideal grounds for consolation and sources of strength may disclose themselves; he will have nothing to do however with "the claim of the ideal" nor the obligations preached by Gregers. Only that which sustains and consoles has validity and should be regarded as true; all "truths" which are incapable of that should be veiled in tranquillizing and bracing illusions. In special cases, it is valid to devise illusions which will serve as painkilling and narcoticizing opiates that permit one to forget the unfairness of life, stimulate human self-esteem and encourage people to believe in their virtues and talents. These as well as serve to hide uncomfortable weaknesses, and to give people lifts for their shoes to make them appear taller than they indeed are. On that account, Relling says to Gregers: "No need to use that foreign word—ideals; we do have a perfectly good Norwegian word for it—lies."

As a good doctor he is well-intentioned in helping his patients, not only in body, but also in mind, as he manufactures lies in the shape of curative pills, dispensing them discriminately according to an individual's need and circumstances. He must fight Gregers, as does a healer against a poisoner; with justification, he asserts, "When you take away his life-lie from the average person, you take away, at the same time, his happiness."

Long practice had taught him that. What he administers naturally, therefore, aims to give everyone consolation and comfort; what Gregers wants is to elevate man. What Dr. Relling tries to provide are stilts and crutches; in contrast, Gregers wants everyone to find wings.

The battleground, so to speak, where the opponents contend, is the home of the photographer and erstwhile artist Hjalmar Ekdal. Gregers assumes that Hjalmar has enjoyed a loving upbringing whereby "the claim of the ideal has not been forgotten." Relling, however, adds that Hjalmar was brought up by "two eccentric and hysteric spinster aunts," his foster "soul mothers," who treated the motherless boy like the star of the future and spoiled him to the limits of their abilities. And so the ideal elements that protected and cultivated his youth also formed gently coddled temptations. His idealism consequently lacked a backbone, remained soulful and rhetorical, and thus led to self-mirroring. An attractive appearance, "handsome, of good color and delicate, the way girls like a boy to be," distinguished him outwardly from his boyhood friend, the ugly Gregers; inwardly, he differed from Gregers' blunt idealism.

When Gregers descends from his isolated mountains after many years and again meets Hjalmar, he thinks that he must shoulder heavy responsibilities for him. Because of his father, the merchant Werle, the Ekdal family had suffered much injustice. The elder Ekdal was exploited through enterprises which plunged him into shame and poverty, while his son Hjalmar was deprived of a career as an artist. But through the seeming generosity of the merchant Werle, he was educated to be a photographer so that he could be married off to Gina, a former mistress of Werle. Despite this deception of her husband, Gina proves to be a courageous and industrious woman. Her diligent work alone keeps the domestic and business activities on track, something Hjalmar shows little concern for. But her tender care constantly envelops him with the sluggish comfort of conventionality, like convenient and soft upholstery upon which his complacency can expand and stretch; and so, all his best strength sinks into a lazy half-slumber. And thanks to Relling's cheer-producing opium pill, Hjalmar's slumber is made pleasant by the dream that he believes himself on the verge of making a great discovery which will bring fame and fortune. The longing for something higher—which still resides in Hjalmar but which is injured by the triviality of his life—expresses itself in a flattering phantom-image, composed of self-satisfied vanity and childish illusions of grandeur. He plays with the phantom image just as does his doddering father who occupies himself with the rubbish and animals in the attic, which replace his previous life and freedom in the forests.

As soon as Gregers is aware of all this, he is determined to

rescue Hjalmar from such an undignified situation. Not through
exhortative moral preachments does he mean to achieve this, but
as a gift-bearer who attempts to rectify the offenses committed
against the Ekdals. He will reveal to Hjalmar that his family life
has been built on the deceptions perpetrated by the merchant
Werle; then he would call upon Hjalmar and Gina to begin a new,
more beautiful life and marriage, with liberating truth. He realizes that whatever Gina contributed to the deception, her in-
dustry and faithfulness put Hjalmar's self-satisfied weakness to
shame; she had done her part, to the best of her ability, to make a
true marriage. Hjalmar, however, must learn that he needs to
contribute his share of forgiving to transform the everyday and
lift their marriage to inspired heights.

In the meantime, Gregers is far from seeing his plan realized,
and his revelations only cause an indescribable, unholy confusion. Certainly, for one moment, Hjalmar gathers all his rhetorical energy to rise to the importance of the hour, but he soon
recalls that he was never accustomed to high style and was not
about to don now a tragic toga; he was more comfortably habituated to a shabby housejacket.

Irritated human passions at first foam with wild anger, and
without a tidal swell from the outside, a stagnating lake temporarily is saved from becoming a sump; only the muck was stirred
up from the deep and sinks back very slowly to the slimy bottom
after a turgid peace had returned. Gregers is as inept in large
matters as he is with the small. As lodger with the Ekdals, his
assertive and misplaced energy in attempting his first lighting of a
stove almost causes a conflagration, and here too the incautiously
stirred-up fire subsides into a foul mixture of dirt and awful odor
that infests the whole house.

To a certain extent, Hjalmar is representative of a cross-
section of humanity through which Gregers gains his tragic
knowledge of life: the knowledge that he completely erred in his
preconceived self-stylization as a bringer of joy and dispenser of
blessings to humans, and instead—like a "hardened fanatic"—
comes to "ram through people's doors" with his "claim of the
ideal." It is the tragic knowledge that his wish to offer all his
precious gifts so generously, could be regarded as thievery, rob-
bing humans of their most important and indispensable

characteristic, namely, the desire to create illusions and mirages. He must learn that with average persons, truth necessarily appears as a thief who takes from them more than they can afford to give; the acceptance of gifts presupposes high capabilities. To the tame wishes of emasculated domestic animals, such gifts and truths appear like something rapacious and predatory. So, it becomes obvious that the harbinger of gifts and truths is hated, feared, and even superstitiously avoided everywhere with horror. At the table of life, the best delicacies are no longer appetizing when one knows that such a sinister harbinger and guest sits at one's side. There remains little else to do for the guest except to creep away silently, as does Gregers, from the happy gathering. When Gregers painfully answers Relling's question, he understands that he is "the thirteenth at the table."

Gregers is overtaken by the same typical fate encountered by the like-minded Dr. Stockmann in Ibsen's *An Enemy of the People*. As a dramatic figure, Stockmann stands closest to Gregers; but whereas his cheerful childishness combines with the battle-tested strength of a Brand without either of their weaknesses, Stockmann rises distinctly above the portrait of an enthusiast for the ideal and is a prototype of genuine manliness. With Ibsen's "enemy of the people," a male appears for the first time next to Ibsen's female figures as the central figure of a play and as a representation of a man as he ought to be.

Gregers' "claim of the ideal" contains common sense and is so self-evident that his environment instead seems to us to be almost inhuman because its lack of communal concern prevents fulfillment of the "claim." Although as a result, ideals and reality hopelessly part from one another, Stockmann by no means gives up his battles and hopes for the future; unlike Gregers, he does not retreat. He feels happiest in the midst "of tumultuous, unquiet life . . . right here, on the plains of battle! . . . Right here, I will win!" He faces a world that reviled him, but he is man enough to know that despite everything he has made an impact.

The inner tie between the apostle of truth and the man of convention, which Stockmann possesses in his self-reliance, exists for Gregers for a time when he finds a young disciple. Hedwig follows him not because of her own ideals but with a shy and trusting hand pressed into his, for she is only a child. Since in this play we have a group of people, unlike other Ibsen dramas in which the individual is the focus, it is significant that here the figure of a child joins the earlier female figures; as such, she can only be understood truly within the framework of her family. But, at the same time, she steps out of the circle of the more general types with such personal warmth and fullness of life that she becomes a tiny figuration of poetry. When the loud din of conflicting opinions finally subsides, gently but perceptibly her child's voice outsounds everything.

Hedwig is Gina's daughter and Hjalmar suspects that she is Gregers' half-sister. In conversation with Gregers, she expresses in her childish ways an artistic disposition—apparently gained from her father—through her delight in drawing pictures, which points to her being Hjalmar's child. But the vacillating light— which purposely obscures her origin—places her on a reconciling median line between Gregers, the idealist, and Hjalmar, the conventional man. In her childish view there is no chasm be-tween Gregers' relentless drive for the truth and Hjalmar's search for illusion. Ensconced in a domestic life that already outwardly characterizes Hjalmar's life-lie, Hedwig grows up amid the poverty-stricken everyday atmosphere of a seedy attic, divided in half by a bare curtain; one part, with its topsy-turvy rag-tags, has been polished until it shines like a world of illusion. In Hedwig's childish joy, the attic room with its fir trees, birds, and hatching baskets is sheer poetry. With trustful respect she looks up to Hjalmar's great phrases because deceptions and lies are com-pletely alien to her.

She does not as yet notice the false and the borrowed, she sees only the rare sunny beams of tender and genuine moods, which glide over Hjalmar's soul, like the sparse rays that occa-sionally transform the rag-tags of the attic room. It is also she, with a tiny and dependent heart, who knows how most often to cull such moods from him. In one scene of the second act, Hed-wig is the one to bring him his flute when Hjalmar is prompted to escape briefly from misery by playing music; the flute playing momentarily silences the false sounds of his life.

If in Hedwig's great love and admiration lie the strongest challenge for Hjalmar to become industrious in order not to shame her expectations, there also lurk dangers for Hedwig.

Precisely the childish dependency, with which all her thoughts and hopes fasten on her father, could suddenly rupture and bring struggle and conflict into the idyllic peace of her childhood. The bright and dazzling colors with which her imagination sees her father are destined to pale suddenly and yield to a confused and lightless darkness. Just so will the progressively worsening eye-disease extinguish forever the bright reflections of the outer world. Unsuspectingly however, "cheerful and carefree and chirping like a little bird, she flutters into the eternal night of life."

With the revelations about his family situation, which Hjalmar receives from Gregers, danger breaks rapidly and un-expectedly over Hedwig. The fact that Gina had been the mer-chant's mistress awakens doubts retrospectively about Hedwig's paternity. She is rejected by Hjalmar and cast aside, without in the least grasping the cause. In her bitter fear of having lost his love, Hedwig takes Gregers' advice to sacrifice what is most dear to her and so regain Hjalmar's love. She will shoot the wild duck, her only possession, which "she loves so anxiously" that she includes it in her evening prayers.

The next day with Ekdal's old pistol in hand, she sneaks into the attic in order to perform her childish sacrifice, when unavoid-ably she hears the horrible conversation in the next room. Hjal-mar's pitiful weakness is expressed in the ineradicable mistrust which he must harbor now against Hedwig's honesty and loyal-ty. She is forced to hear that not only has he ceased to love her but that because of his suspicions and doubts, her very existence will prevent his prospective achievements. When Gregers in-dignantly defends Hedwig, Hjalmar replies with the sarcastic question as to whether or not Hedwig would waver one moment in choosing the merchant and living in luxury or choosing Hjal-mar and dying for him in poverty.

The question receives an immediate reply through a loud pistol shot from the attic. Not against the beloved wild duck, but against herself was it directed. It was the answer wrung from helpless anguish and indescribable pain—a deadly, gruesome answer. And yet, it was a decisive and clear answer which de-clared that she was his child, his bodily child and never anything except that, exclusively his with her total child's being unto death; at the same time, her answer made it clear that she had different values and that in spirit, she was related to Gregers.

This surprising turn away from the wild duck to herself, from sacrifice to self-sacrifice, is not odd, even though Hedwig is young and imbued with the sparkle of life. The fact is that she finds herself in the danger-filled years of transition—during pubescence and adolescent sentimentality—or the years, which Relling warningly notes, "when the voice changes."

Gina tells us something characteristic about Hedwig: in the kitchen, she busies herself strangely with the glowing coals, and when sparks fly she calls it "playing at house-on-fire." She is at the age when that which still was child's play now already borders on seriousness, where play foreshadows the lighting of fire and sparks—a constant danger. Nowhere is the decisive and critical turn so closely linked with the guileless and childish. It is the time when, as in spring, the earth's surface is soft and charmingly decorated with innocuous flowers, while tremors begin to disturb the depths. Over the peaceful fairytales and ideals of her young being, a squall breaks out, at first caressing like the winds of March caress the violets, but then picking up in fury and rapidly swelling into storms that upheave the seas and uproot the trees.

In nature it is the time when the precious flowerstalks are still enveloped by light and warming hulls, so that when the sun penetrates their tender and rare buds, they will blossom. And it is the time when something, which has lain dreaming in a human soul, needs the most tender touch and care. What was done to Hedwig resembles brutality that forcibly explodes all the tender hulls wherein life germinates, unborn, in sacred and protective darkness. It is like the callous grip of a fist that exposes the most naked and helpless and tears it out as a death offering.

At any rate, things occur unintentioned and completely unpredicted. Hedwig's nature, shaped for the true and genuine, takes in deadly earnest what merely are empty phrases and grand rhetoric. And so, she answers with a real, deadly accurate shot, in an environment behind whose curtains occur calculated sham shots, sham hunts, and sham wildlife. That pistol which had already pointed waveringly at the breast of the elder and the young Ekdal, without ever discharging, fulfills in Hedwig's childlike hand the only seriously intended and definitive act amid the illusion-veiled life of Ekdal. It is an act committed by one whose nature is like that of a wild bird inhabiting the attic. And if the shot had not proven fatal, her recovery and existence would be filled with the same unmeasurable loneliness as that of a captive wild bird.

Even Gregers' hope that Hedwig's death finally "will set free what is noble" in Hjalmar, and that her pistol shot will smash the hollow theatrical world, are hopes that do not come to fruition. The effect upon him of her death has no louder resonance than the rapid fading of the pistol's sharp report, which for a moment reverberates in the human nervous system but is unable to transform anyone. One cannot help but speculate along with Relling that "before nine months are over, little Hedwig will be nothing to Hjalmar except a pretty theme for declamation."

Hedwig's corpse is not of the kind over which two radically different opponents, like Hjalmar and Gregers, clasp hands in a lifelong bond. And yet one can attribute to her suicide an inner meaning that contains the elements for their reconciliation and communication.

It is as if that sacrificial shot drowns out whatever could stir in Gregers' breast—contempt for humans and inconsolability. It is as if Hedwig had wished to give proof that the challenge and advice given by the young, untainted Gregers did not appear to her as totally strange and impossible, and that she enthusiastically received him not as a hard fanatic, but as a joyous emissary. Life's complications, burdens, and dulling effects slowly broke and choked one's strength and originality, rendering it artificial. Thousands upon thousands of sprouting seeds would have to languish before a resigned longing for comfortable crutches and artificial uplifts would yield to a desire for liberation. Indeed, the habitual wish alone for consoling and deceptive illusions, whereby a person stands upright, is often nothing else than a distortion and fashioning of the same longing that seeks ascendance over the workaday crassness of things, striving toward truth and freedom, and realizing correctly that the borrowed crutches are only broken and maimed uplifters.

If that is so, then something may lie even in the distortions and maimings, which can grip and move one as much as a disfigurement in a well-proportioned face. For something also rests over Hjalmar who is at the mercy of weaknesses and self-deception; in his expression, there is something that prevents him from becoming a comic figure, an expression that merits our sadness and sympathy. Through Hedwig's pious beliefs as a child, with which she—blindly, though perhaps divinely prophetic—clings to her father, during her young life and into death, there arises from the caricature a figure of the tragically human.

In that sense, Hedwig's death is testimony for Hjalmar and the average man against the hard idealism of Gregers. Beside the harshness of those ideals stands her trusting confidence which desires to help rather than to judge. Touchingly, she expresses all this in childlike words, answering Gregers' question of whether or not she wishes to go out into the world and grow up free: "I want to be home always to help father and mother."

She sees the realization of her greatest wish in quietly helping her family, not in emancipating herself from the circle of her family. In that, she resembles Stockmann's daughter, Petra, whose greatest love and hope, despite her vigorous independence, are summed up at the end of the play with the outcry, "Father!" Circumstances in that play dictate that a man be the dominating figure, while in *The Wild Duck* it is a female figure, Hedwig.

Although Petra's role in Ibsen's social drama *An Enemy of the People* is not quite in the foreground, it does have a characteristic trait which also gives importance to Hedwig: Petra demonstrates through her dedication and courageous support of her father that Stockmann is right in his unshakeable belief in humanity.

And so it is, this time as well, that female figures pick up and carry forward the basic thoughts of Ibsen's earlier dramas, particularly the theme of reconciling the ideal and the real through an all-comprehending and all-forgiving perception of truth. Even if the idealized demand for truth is embodied in Gregers, only Hedwig's life and death add those elements whereby an abstract dream becomes a force in human existence. Relying solely upon himself, Gregers succumbs to the power of reality, just as did his ideological predecessor Brand. Here, it is the child Hedwig's voice which calls out the words to Gregers that Brand heard from the heavens, when he lay dying, words that condemned his hardness: "He is *Deus caritatis*!"

With such an interpretation, Hjalmar becomes human for us

in the light of Hedwig's freely-given love and the forbiddingly strict Gregers, a figure of the ideal. Hjalmar and Gregers approach each other but then their paths take opposite directions. Although it seems that Hjalmar's path leads upward to Gregers, we learn in fact that Gregers' heads down to Hjalmar's level. Gregers is incapable of truly filling the chasm between his claims of the ideal and human nature, and he is unable to understand and shape the world he wanted to transform. Therein lies the reason why Gregers' pure idealism moves one step closer to the dishonest phraseologies of a Hjalmar.

With Relling's victory over the "fanatic truth-demander," the point is made that an ideal must project its inner truth and especially shun estrangement from life and the disparagement of it. In brief, the preacher Gregers, with his repetitive sermon-text about obligations to the ideal, must first prove that with his message he knows how to become a true physician to mankind, instead of a thoughtless mischief-maker. The medicine may be precious and one's aim may have the best intention, but in the hand of the inexperienced, they are dangers that bring death instead of life. Without motivation or enthusiasm for the ideal, Relling—as Gregers cannot—sees his task very much like that of the fully qualified Dr. Stockmann, namely, to be a physician in the service of mankind. And although Relling's sugar-coated pills and his less than noble aims cannot succeed in healing, but only in plastering over wounds and artificially stimulating sinking powers; nevertheless, he achieves more than Gregers. The "thirteenth at a table" is merely the one who is found to be completely superfluous.

Ibsen's Gregers figure has been criticized as being too abstract. But only if that figure were to represent an ideal type would that criticism be justified; that is, if the playwright were to identify his own idealism with that of Gregers'. In other respects, the abstract ideal tendency appears precisely as Gregers' human weakness, a weakness which Dr. Stockmann transcends to come much closer to the ideally human. Gregers' image only hovers over life; it is not rooted in it, but glides by—out of darkness and into darkness. All this harbors Ibsen's verdict pronounced on Gregers.

Nevertheless it seems that his traits appear again with an

uncanny and distorted resemblance. These no longer represent unspoiled enthusiasm but are features devastated and furrowed by the experiences and the sufferings throughout a long life; it is no longer the figure of Gregers in the first flush of youth, but one coming from a long and useless journey, dusty, unkempt and with a touch of the vagabond. That figure is Ulric Brendel in Ibsen's *Rosmersholm*.

In Ibsen's next play, Brendel like Gregers is a representative of a disposition that has escaped the tight reins of the ideal in order to roam in the hoboland of the ideal and freedom. Gregers in the purely abstract, whose life does not stand in full relief, embodies, so to speak, the spirit of the female figures discussed so far in an extreme ideal form. Just so, in the restless roaming of Brendel is mirrored the mind of Rebecca and Ellida, the lady of the sea.

Like Gregers, Brendel in his youthful enthusiasm naïvely gave himself over to the ideals of freedom and truth; like him, he fled from the tumult of life into isolation in order to dedicate himself to mankind. And like Gregers, he triumphs over himself and returns to real life, teaching and preaching in a world he sees dominated by impurity. He prepares himself as for a sacrificial feast for which he will offer what is most precious to him. But, he experiences something strange, as did Gregers when he wanted to transform Hjalmar's family life through his ideals: as soon as his ideals came too close in contact with reality, they evaporated into hapless failure.

Brendel's disappointment comes about through a conversation with the editor of a radical periodical which he wishes to join. Peter Mortensgaard's experiences led him to choose a cautious middle-ground and he advises Brendel that the real secret of action and success lies in the "living of life without ideals."

Brendel, however, does not have it in him to surrender his most priceless ideas. Just as Gregers leaves life with stolid resignation after his great tragic understanding, so Brendel follows his great longing for annihilation after his most sacred possessions have melted into nothingness.

Seen more accurately, the effect of life's lesson, as well as the reason for his dying, is completely different from Gregers' situation. Through the immense contrast between his ideals and real-

ity, Gregers gains the insight that people do not have the capability of raising themselves up to ideals. For that reason, he abandons the field of battle; yet for him the truth and purity of the ideal
remain completely untouched, although it has not come to fruition. In contrast, Brendel's inner confidence is shaken. With
bitter derision, he begs Rosmer for a few "old, used ideals," just
as earlier he had pleaded for old boots and clothes. For "just as I
was ready to empty my horn-of-plenty, I made the painful discovery that I was bankrupt. . . . During twenty-five years I sat
like a miser in front of his locked money vault. And then yester-
day, when I wanted to open it and remove the treasure, nothing
was there. . . . Nothing, absolutely nothing was left."

And so he also becomes impoverished inwardly, a beggar,
uprooted and crushed, as already evident in his outer appearance. Gregers though is undeterred and now—as before—he is
an implacably hard ruler in the realm of the ideal, whose naked-
ness and poverty he tries to hide with his regal clothes.

That kind of poverty though is intolerable to Brendel. The
nobility of his mind cannot survive it, because that poverty would
reduce him to such burning shame as no bedraggled dress could.
He dies for that reason.

And yet, the deepest cause for his sad bankruptcy lies in
something disorderly, patched, and torn that already characterized his enthusiasm from the beginning. Something in his liberation and drive for truth caused him to be impulsive and obstinate,
making him appear intoxicated and tipsy, and earning for him the
stigma of vagrancy.

His ideals do not really constitute life-nourishment, nor do
they produce strong and healthy sustenance for creative pleasure
and work. Rather, his ideals are nothing more than nibbling and
gourmandizing. "You know," he says to Rosmer, a former clergyman, "I have a touch of the sybarite and gourmet, all my life
long. . . . I have gorged myself with such bliss on my secret
visions, a bliss of dizzying heights. . . . Why should I profane my
ideals if I can enjoy them privately and with purity?"

With these raptures and dreams within an ideal world of
fantasy that serves his own comfort and pleasure, Brendel is so
far removed from Gregers that he reminds one almost of Hjalmar.
In Brendel, both these human types cross marvelously well, and

with deep meaning. One can follow distinctly the fine lines as they entwine and become fused in a single, tragic human configuration. Hjalmar and Brendel descend the steps, so to speak, on either side of the temple of pure ideality, where Gregers reigns as priest. On one side of the temple, we see an idealism that does not dare rise to its full power and height; it does not accept the challenge of freedom and the truthful life, and instead of the temple, it searches for a protective and sheltering theater chamber in which to construct a decorative, artificial world of illusion into whose half-darkness no harsh light or cold air can enter. There, fantasies can give themselves over to unrestrained dreams. On the other side of the temple of ideality, protest against prejudice, barriers and the narrowing of the drive to freedom can only lead to vagabondage. Although idealism really was born as well on Gregers' terrain, it tramps about aimlessly from one idea to another and from one adventure to another, without being able to bring itself to enter into the strict and bounded domain of the temple whose priest he claims to be.

Not only do the inner connections or fine-veined relationships place Hjalmar and Brendel significantly beside Gregers but they also assume a very specific position in the totality of the six Ibsen plays discussed in this book. In one respect, all three differ from figures discussed so far: they are the first in whom deficiencies and weaknesses no longer are emphasized as deriving from the dangers of heredity and the chains of convention; on the contrary, they derive from the absence of chains and from free will. Already in Gregers' obligation to the ideal lies something which goes beyond the emancipation of Nora and Mrs. Alving. Poised against Hjalmar's ideal—the release toward freedom—and his weakness is not the shaping of an independent personality through rigid, outside compulsion, but, on the contrary, his complacent and despotic delusion of grandeur; he has no serious insight. Here lie his self-indulgence and his misuse of freedom, instead of conscious and strict submission to truth, once it is manifest.

In that respect, the male triad stands at the center of the plays, as if two lines of development converged and were hardly noticeable in a common center. Brendel stands on the threshold of a further development which, however, is picked up and spun out by female figures. And yet, when the "vagabond-apostle" Brendel replaces the "apostle of ideal severity" Gregers, he appears as a characteristic companion of these women because they do not, like their forerunners, obtain their education in an attic and other narrow confines, but in the wildness of shackle-free and unconstrained rovings. In the long run, therefore, they pursue an opposite goal: for them, unlike Nora or Mrs. Alving, the liberation from servility cannot serve as an ideal inducement because they are in greater need of taming and reining-in in order to achieve their highest potential; their uncontrolled, tumbling, unpruned energy and drives need refinement and control. If their forerunners first achieved a complete, inner victory through emancipation, so here the victory of full self-development is marked by submission and self-sacrifice. One may already note that precisely with those women who are free of shackles, the power and mission of their love must assume an entirely different form of expression than that of their predecessors. Nora and Mrs. Alving also love, and they love unhappily, but their deepest motive is delusion, an erroneous glorification of the lover, a confusion of his and their own notions of ideal existence. In order to gain freedom and an understanding of the truth, they must battle to tear themselves away from that kind of love. With Ibsen's subsequent female figures, on the contrary, we find that in their love, for the first time, the sacramental ties dissolve. These women attain consciousness and control of themselves in that they sacrifice the self; they do not idealize the man who is the object of their love, but they idealize their own love, and their still obscure ideals evaporate in contact with that man and his conception of life.

In the area between these diametrically opposed female types and between their lines of development, we see little Hedwig sitting at the feet of Gregers. From one perspective, she is related to Nora and Mrs. Alving because she too derives from the narrowness of an attic, and with Gregers' hand she strives toward another abode. If Hedwig were not a child, she would have consciously emancipated herself from the humans who encircled her, a circle from which she is freed by death; her act would have resembled that of the instinctive nature of a wild bird.

But she still is a child, and that means being able only to

experience her growing self in a trustful nestling close to her father and in her devoted love for him. Hedwig's attitude points to a transition toward the next group of Ibsen's female figures. The sacrifice brought about by her love becomes the epitome of her childish stature—and with that, it becomes clear in what point the new line of development is to culminate: the giving of one's self instead of the freeing of one's self.

Hedwig's first representative is Rebecca.

IV REBECCA

> *"Is it you who follows me or do I follow you?"*
> —Rebecca

> *"We go together, Rebecca . . . because now we two are one."*
> —Rosmer

S HE WAS BORN in the highlands of Finnmark. By nature she was a free spirit of the wilds, whose unpredictable and sudden storms ridiculed society's codes of behavior. And so, she also is the child of a rapidly igniting and fleeting passion, engendered outside the pale of convention. Rebecca owes her birth to the fleeting familiarity of the district midwife, Mrs. Gamwik, with a Dr. West who passed through the area. After her mother's death, she is adopted by Dr. West and is reared in the freethinking atmosphere fostered by him. The secret of her origin is kept from her, and consequently she grows up to be an attractive and strong girl; she is misled into the same intimate relationship which her mother had with Rebecca's father.

Rebecca's youth was shaped in deepest contrast to the influences that marked Nora's and Helene Alving's upbringing. The usual biases which blocked their development are alien to her, but at the same time, so are tender pampering, and protective, solicitous influences. Essentially, it is this kind of protectiveness that permitted Nora to step into marriage so childlike, pure and untouched, carrying over her admiration—like a tender, unconscious ideal—for her father into her love as a wife. This forms the tragic conflict, no less than the inner starting point, for her mature development during her later life; she fights to come into her own and to discard the deficiencies and distortions of her upbringing. In its deepest sense, the *childlike* is the power that releases her from the *childish*. For all this, there is no room within the brutal experiences of Rebecca's youth; even natural and childlike piety is spurred to sensual arousal within her. And just as in *A Doll's House*, the loved one rises almost to the stature of a venerated father, so here in *Rosmersholm* the father sinks to the level of a lover.

And when—similarly demeaning—the "wonder" of fatefully destructive love breaks over Mrs. Alving in *Ghosts*, what is it that ultimately allows her to rise above it with calm dignity? It is not the drive and longing for freedom and truth alone, but the strength of her spirit, as well as the fusion of freedom and truth into an ideal through which she sacrifices all personal happiness in order to cope with the reality of life. In Mrs. Alving's and Nora's emancipation, freedom and truth signify the highest goal—a peak, while in Rebecca's youth, these are represented by a flat, luxuriant land on which all her impulses tumble around with untamed abandon. In their interiors, therefore, lie these characteristics, undifferentiated in value. These live on with the wild innocence of a naïve egoism which is as little ashamed as the first human in Paradise, where the human and the animalistic rested together peacefully; there, the guiding and dominant power of egoism still remained alien and unconscious. With that alone, one can explain that already in Rebecca's early life and spirit, the most unassimilable elements are naïvely united—an instinctive and piety-filled thankfulness, and sensual precocity—the lamb with the lion. And further, although she has unchained herself prematurely through a robust and self-seeking strength, she has done it with the friendly patience of a daughter who endures a foster-father and his whims, and who lessens his pains until he dies.

The death of Dr. West forces Rebecca to look in the outside world for her fortune because she had inherited nothing except an old box filled with books. But she applies herself to the task with confident courage. The great world which opens before her does not frighten her but only stimulates and spurs her powers, for she knows how advantageous a preparation for battle and fortune it is to be strong and unbiased in regard to pleasures, and not to fear anything. With that, she wins almost instantly the friendship of an influential sponsor, the rector Kroll, who brings her into the home of his brother-in-law, Pastor Rosmer, to care for Kroll's sickly sister, Beate. As yet, Kroll is unaware of the contrast he himself represents to Rebecca's untamed nature. He only senses in her that with which he has an affinity—her brave and strong being whose integral unity and sound health are grounded in self-reliance; both possess a massive strength rather than a fine sensitivity.

But precisely, this resolute energy gained for Kroll a far-reaching influence over Rosmersholm; since his marriage, Rosmer bends to him as willingly as he had submitted to an entirely opposite spirit and will during his boyhood when the radical free-spirit and fantasizing idealist, Ulric Brendel, was his household teacher for a short time. In Rosmer, it is the faithful dependency upon laws and custom which encouraged his adaptability to the transmitted and consequent laming of will, preventing his independent development. Just as the painted portraits of the deceased peer down from the walls upon the living heirs, so Rosmer mainly spent his life under the scrutiny of the dead, and in silent reverence for the deceased. Never then does his strength awaken him to stand equal, or superior, to his ancestors; under their pressures, there only develop fine, devotional inclinations—a tenderness of spirit and mood—which like simple wreaths of immortality and brooding seriousness are intended to pay homage to the venerated pictures of the dead.

As soon as Rebecca steps into Rosmersholm territory, she realizes that it must be quite simple to be able to dominate and conquer. In her individualism are united both powers to which Rosmer had already and willingly submitted—the lordly power of Kroll as well as the rabble-rousing intellectual bent of Brendel. While in this sense she succeeds in influencing him, leading his will and stimulating his mind, she also wins the heart of his wife, Beate. Of a fine and sensitive disposition, Beate is the feminine counterpart of Rosmer, and with respect to Rebecca she even finds herself "on the border of falling in love." She feels overwhelmed by the assured and unbounded strength exuded by Rebecca's total personality, and as if stunned, she helplessly falls under her spell. What is reflected is less an attraction to love than hypnosis, less obedience through persuasion than through suggestiveness. And therefore, that relationship does not change, even when Rebecca's manner of action awakens hurt, jealousy and horror in Beate; her boundless superiority over this tender and timorous creature draws its nourishment from fear as well as from love.

There slumbers in Rebecca a wildness that resembles a beast of prey at rest and which hungers for spoil. For the time being, she is fully satisfied with herself, and from her free, satiated power streams a fresh breath of nature—that enlivens and intoxicates—throughout the melancholy coldness of the Rosmer domicile. As yet, her influence is as barely perceived as is the effect of the sumptuous, decorative flower bouquets which she carries into the old-fashioned rooms; and with flower blossoms she attempts, indeed, to hide the great, stolid tile-stove, a morose reminder of snow and winter. And like Rebecca herself, her flowers—with their unusual and lively glow of colors, with their warm and secretly penetrating odor—worked variedly, but effectively, upon Rosmer as well as Beate. The flowers attracted him mysteriously, almost with the premonition of a happier and more colorful life; while they had an opposite effect upon Beate, who was bewildered and made fearful, until finally they made her ill.

The tranquillity of Rebecca was suddenly disrupted by the intrusion of something catastrophic. A wild, unrestrained passion for Rosmer seized her senses. "It came over me like a storm out of the sea," as she described it, "like one of those storms which we have up North right around winter time. It takes hold of one . . . and carries one away . . . as far as it wishes. No resistance is possible."

The fateful cloud under which she was born, the surroundings in which she grew up, the sensual, sultry atmosphere enfolding her youth, and all of her early experiences with their implications and consequences now burst through. The peaceful condition of primal, paradisiacal innocence—where lamb and lion lay down together—now changes, with the storm of passion, into all the horrors and dangers of a wilderness. Within all this, the exposed human who has no self-awareness as yet also possesses no assertive command over the unchained forces. The only power which still slumbers within Rebecca is a governing and reflective self-control; though strong in everything, she is powerless in the face of the forces that break out of her.

So, her passions surge ahead unhindered, through the irresistibility of her own instinct. What she mustered to secure influence and position over Rosmersholm, and to free Rosmer intellectually, now becomes the means for conquest through her passion. It is evident that two things separate her from his love: his God and his wife.

However, before she succeeds in estranging him from his

religious beliefs, she uses this cautiously anticipated change in
order to awaken mistrust and unease in Beate. The notion that the
religious Rosmer could become untrue to the beliefs of his youth
could lend greater credibility to the next suspicion that he could
be untrue to his wife. In order to make all this appear not only as
natural, but also as almost his inalienable right, Rebecca slips into
Beate's hands books in which childlessness is portrayed as the
destruction of the intrinsic sense and purpose of marriage. Incapable of defending herself against Rebecca's insinuations and influences, Beate is tortured and martyred, but involuntarily follows Rebecca until completely shattered nerves deprive her of the
sole weapon she possesses—her husband's affection. Her wild
self-recrimination, her loud grief, and the near-irrational passion
with which Beate clings to Rosmer in order to compel him to her,
all act to repel his sensitive nature from something painful and
unreasonable.

While in this fashion the selfless purity of Beate's love is
distorted into wild and painful features, Rebecca's sensual glow
is suffused and shows in an earnest and mildly spiritualized face,
a face upon which, as she knows, Rosmer's eyes like to linger
lovingly. Although she has no power over her aroused drives,
still she has enough presence of mind to use an inner self-
restraint to come closer to her objectives. It is the natural
cunning—the soft paw and sleek bearing—of an animal filled
with ravenous greed as it softly circles its prey. Her manoeuver
may almost be compared with an act of nature, and more and
more takes on the character of the elementally driving as she is
caught up in her own actions. She is like a whipped-up sea which
constantly opens up abysses that must drag down everything
near. Nothing can, so to speak, walk on the waters and soothe
them. Her own self veers rudderless, with the passivity of a
horror-stricken person numb with fear; she is an almost impartial
observer of the ferocious play of her passions and is in danger of
perishing through them. And so, she struggles with the desperation of a drowning person, with Beate aboard a foundering life-
boat. "It was," she said, "like a battle in the boatkeel with Beate
and myself."

She acted with a blind and irresistible necessity—or, more
accurately, an inner compulsion acted itself out—as she pretends

to Beate that something has happened which forces her immediately to give up her post at Rosmersholm. In the firm belief that Rebecca has already usurped her place and received that token which had been denied to her own childless marriage, the miserably sick Beate is left also to her own devices in the last conflict.

Only to her brother, the rector, does she point out: "Soon I will die, and now I do not have much time any more, for as soon as possible Rosmer must marry Rebecca." In her sick thoughts and in her kind heart, she persuades herself to clear a place for both of them. Early discipline and rigorous religious beliefs had purged all animal-like desires; never could she feel hatred or revenge toward Rebecca. Helplessly, silently, she wrapped herself in great toleration and forgivingness, and through suicide celebrates her quiet victory over her rival—in the millstream.

Though far removed from the truth as were Rebecca's insinuations which drove Beate to her death, they were not devoid of a certain foundation. In his deep sympathy with the unhappy Beate, Rosmer believes that insanity had snatched her away prematurely, but her passing, after so many tortured years, permits him at the same time to breathe with relief and release. The anxiety-producing agitations have vanished, and again he is surrounded by a contemplative silence consonant with his nature; but it is no longer the dejecting, dead silence of earlier times, for an enlivening and releasing spirit now fills the silence, which now has a cheerful aspect. All constricting bonds slowly fall away from him; as unreservedly as he had followed Kroll, he subordinates his will and spirit to Rebecca's more fervently than he had listened to Brendel's teachings. And Rebecca's awareness that his happiness and fortune rested with her, acts soothingly on her recollection of the horror that had to occur in order to make possible his new life. All her hopes seem about to be fulfilled. Rosmer becomes a freethinker; he gives up his preacher's office and thinks about carrying, with Rebecca's help, his joyous and liberating message to the people who would be ennobled and made happy.

In the course of time, Rebecca insinuates herself so well into Rosmer's lofty, mild way of thinking that slowly the painful impatience of her passions was calmed. Not in vain does she stand at the side of Rosmer, for her guidance causes whatever is unchained and aimless in his disposition to change involuntarily into a positive ideal and to an enthusiastic mission, that aims to bring people help, joy and reconciliation. Not in vain does his soul open to her during their daily living together, with all its hidden moods and stirrings, "so fine and tender in his feelings." And eventually something strange happens to her.

"Ever so slowly, it came. Almost unnoticeably but finally so overpoweringly, down to the depths of my soul." She seemed like a hunter who daringly has battled for his prey, and now that he stands directly in front of it and observes its delicate beauty, the hunter's outstretched arms slowly sink. Silently moved, he remains stock-still and must wait until all rapacious demands dissolve into sentiment and admiration, and the covetous glance becomes a soundless, deep viewing.

So it is with Rebecca who wanted to steal that grand, guileless soul; another love takes possession of her, free from the earlier sensual greed, but in time equally overwhelming—a deep, invincible passion for the childlike soul of this man. His weakness teaches her how very much tradition and prejudice unnerve one's strength; so, she sees for the first time the inner nobility a person achieves, as the force of the ideal tames the coarser drives. For Rebecca, an untrammeled child of nature who had only heard voices from within a spiritual wilderness—like the pounding of wildly surging rivers, there now suddenly peal the tender, fine tones of a spiritual life which is harmoniously attuned to the perfect pitch of the ear of conscience.

Like a tentative countervoice, touching and gripping, out of the depths of her own soul, it comes over her as if an aeolian harp were carried through a stormy wilderness and its strings were sounded by nature to become strange sounds of wonder. "All these unleashed forces settled into calmness. A blissful peace came over me . . . a silence like that upon one of our high mountains under the midnight sun."

She was as peaceful and quiescent as once before when she blossomed like an untouched flower in the spaciousness of nature, but now she also has become conscious and transcends both the nature-life of the flower and the animalistic; she is uplifted by the wonder of an unforgettable impression on the heights of

humankind. What she celebrates mutely and lonely on this tranquil peak is her awakening to human transcendency, with all her
strength linked to the ideal powers.

But her desire to seize upon and possess Rosmer has dissolved and the sense and goal of her life become unsettled. What
once was her passionate expectation is hardly her hope any
longer; it has flowed into shy and pensive melancholy with which
she humbly waits to see if Rosmer will ever cross over the grave in
the mill-stream to reach her.

Ibsen's masterly portraiture at the beginning of the first act
contains the exposition for the entire situation at Rosmersholm:
Rebecca sits at the window, and with timorous expectation peers
out at Rosmer, who is approaching the house by way of the path
by the mill. On her lap lies a woollen shawl which she crochets,
which is almost finished, except for a few meshes. And during
the long time she continues mesh by mesh, she does not suspect
that she is working on her death shroud which will envelop her
when she dies. It is a symbol of her life's work. With a sad heart,
she already sees that even this time, Rosmer does not dare cross
the stream's footbridge; he takes a detour. His entire being lies in
his hesitation: a brooding and indecisive piety and a ruminative
fear. For that reason, worried words steal from Rebecca's lips:
"Here at Rosmersholm one clings long to the dead!"

A sinister answer that reflects a countryside superstition
comes from the mouth of the domestic manageress, Mrs.
Helseth: "I think that it is the dead who cling to Rosmersholm!
. . . Yes, yes! It's almost as if they really cannot part from those
who are left behind!"

That sounds like the prophetic voice of a ghost. To Rosmer's
persistent weakness, Rebecca responds with mere pensive
melancholy, while that is also embodied in the superstition of an
inherited portrait of an approaching and unavoidable ghostly
power. And like a shadow cast by events, the drowned Beate
glides by ghostly, like a heavy dream-image.

Indeed, first here does the tragedy of Rosmersholm enter into
the drama. It rises with Beate's shadow, and could just as well
have been called "Beate's Revenge" or "Beate's Return." For what
lies in this superstitious representation, literally viewed, we see
again mirrored later in the tragic occurrences in Rebecca's spirit.

The defenseless and conquered Beate was thoughtlessly smashed down, as with a fist, by Rebecca, who acted with the brutal right of the stronger person. Beate not only had to abandon happiness and her realm but, in a deeper and more comprehensive sense with her departure, she opened up, as Rebecca knew and wished, Rosmer's innermost soul, his most secret and fine life. Indeed, even more, she had to permit the outer events that eventually saw Rebecca, through Rosmer's influence, take over all the tender and handsome features of a Beate into her own wild passion, replacing her in a double sense. The deceased also left her a last and sacred bequest: Beate permitted Rebecca to assume completely, with all inner consequences, the place she had vacated.

When Rebecca is about to assume that place, she loses her earlier vigorous strength. Hardly had she rested in blissful silence after her victory, when all her weapons are wrested from her— the brash thievery and the ruthless demand for happiness. She no longer will have anything to do with her former well-armored and weaponed self, for a sense of self-forgetting has come over her and she is able to be happy only within that. If the old self would reappear to her as integral, she would be filled with revulsion and horror at its actions and crudities; she would have to reject and destroy it because it would be directed against her. In sum, if Beate would now return, she would find Rebecca defenseless and at her mercy.

The new blossoming of the mind and the ennoblement which Rebecca had attained also have the fateful disadvantage of no longer having firm footing on her own ground. She is in the thrall of a compulsive attraction to alien ideals. Rebecca cannot absorb all this into a necessary development of her personality because it overtakes her after her personality had been molded and had matured. Already her development and the past lay behind her; all the higher and nobler stirrings which had remained neglected and were pushed back within her now take their revenge. Here is something fateful: while the missing ideals appear to her in an alien perspective rather than as part of her own life-formulation, she cannot think of realizing them except in an alien way. For that reason, the tension and elevation of her mind form, at the same time, its sickness and weakening, and therefore the sacred passion whereby the noblest in her is enflamed signifies also a tragic passion.

Through their mutual influences, Rosmer and Rebecca exchange the highest gifts of love; yet these are fatal gifts. They are unable to fully join and complement each other; they simply infect each other. For Rosmer, the supposedly releasing power remains a dream vision that lives not in himself but beside him in Rebecca's figure. And for Rebecca, the spirit of Rosmersholm can never become a healthy spirit for her own life. It can only sneak into her like something without power to suffuse her and organically transform her being; it is like a bloodless ghost, an alien spirit which roams within her—like Beate's spirit. The deceased cannot assume life within her, and gains only an eerie ghostlike presence which Rebecca's earlier confident and strong being is able to eject; that presence, however, takes away Rosmer's well-being and health.

That kind of necessary inner tragedy is mirrored in Mrs. Helseth's superstitious words about the return of Beate. And barely had she spoken them, when already there nears the first messenger of the conjured-up shadow—Beate's brother, Rector Kroll, who unknowingly ushers in the tragedy.

Since the death of his sister, Kroll had for some time not visited Rosmersholm because he did not wish to serve as a reminder of the terrible suicide; perhaps also because he had a more definite feeling, than did Rosmer himself, that Beate's suicide had to come as a relief and release for Rosmer. All the more then is he honestly touched during his first conversations by the apparent attempt of Rosmer and Rebecca to preserve the memory of his sister. But while this prompts him to reactivate his friendship with Rosmer by challenging him to join in work for a church newspaper, Kroll has his first view of the full change in Rosmer's way of thinking. Such a change and desertion of the flag represent for a person like Kroll a complete break with his brother-in-law. Yet once more, he recollects Beate's last words to him before her death, and the suspicion surfaces in him that above all Rebecca bears the guilt. Now that he knows Rosmer no longer to be a believer, he also speculates about his relationship with Rebecca and speaks openly.

Even though Rosmer indignantly rejects Kroll's interpreta-

tion of Beate's suicide-fall into the millstream, it does not fail to
make a terrifying impression upon him. For the first time, he
imagines that not perhaps through madness, but through the
torture of a frightening suspicion, did she plunge into the water.
Unanchored, he moodily reasons himself into a vision of her
lonely lamentation and struggle, her joyous sacrificial dying for
his sake; and with that, all the carefreeness and life-spirit which
Rebecca had encouraged in him threatened to go under. When
she sees that and senses that even her influence shatters on his
sickly self-torture, very slowly a frosty shudder also overwhelms
her. The past arises anew, and it arises before her, not only in her
own painful memories, but also in the images constantly projected by Rosmer's fear-inspired sensitive fantasy; that fantasy
speaks with his voice, and she views it through his eyes.

Actually she feels no pangs of remorse. Her entire mental
orientation does not develop out of remorse but out of habituation and weakening of will; when she felt the lessening of her
sensual passions, she became no penitent or sinner but an exhausted sufferer. Remorse can only be genuine insofar as
transformation becomes real, calling forth regret of an action,
though one may be still attracted to it. But Rebecca has not truly
been transformed into a new self—only her old self is weakened
and alienated from herself through the ghostly power of a foreign
spirit. She experiences a "horror of the ghost," a horror of seeing
herself die. It is no symptom of change but a dissolution of
personality.

And it is precisely this which makes Rebecca's relationship
with Rosmer so hopeless. He destroys the possibility of ever
burying the past: either the power of Rosmersholm's spirit would
assert itself in her—for then she would be subjected to the terror
of her own annihilation—or she would be able to overcome
everything, and through love strive toward good fortune—for
then she would be the Rebecca of old. Only as the old Rebecca
would she possess moments of health, desire and life, through
which she could escape from passivity and the sloughs of despondency. Almost to the end, and despite her change of mind,
something of her old self continues to steal into every lively
participation and into active expression. Therefore we see two
diametrically opposed phenomena, which follow directly when

Rosmer finally courts Rebecca and finally decides "to pose a life-rich reality against the dead past" in order to free himself from self-torture. At first, a cry of jubilation rushes to his lips, but then just as spontaneously, a "no" wrests itself from her. She is no longer capable of being happy. The boldness with which her crude fist had wished to seize happiness is no longer even able to extend the trembling hand in order to receive it as a gift.

At this moment, Beate's revenge is completed. On the field of battle where Rebecca's force had triumphed, she is ever so quietly drawn over onto Beate's own territory, which ostensibly she had completely vacated. There, however, Rebecca stands without weapons, because in the sacred precinct of selfless and renunciating love, there are no weapons.

But this is not the last satisfaction that accrues to Beate; Rebecca will not only be conquered completely and be incapacitated, but also will submit voluntarily and admit her defeat.

After Rosmer's wooing, she sees his self-recriminations mount and his moodiness increase; she must listen to the suspicions he harbors against himself, namely, that his love for her had already faintly existed from the very beginning of his friendship and was correctly perceived within Beate's sickly premonitions. And so it was, after all, that his unconscious complicity had driven her into death. When Rebecca is witness to Rosmer's innocent and childlike spirit which tortures him with imagined transgressions that become exclusively her burden, she decides to save him through an open confession that would give him back a tranquil conscience. At the same time, this confession is intended to prove the ennobling effect he has had upon her and how great therefore his capability of edifying people.

Nowhere does Rebecca appear to have changed more uncannily into a Beate than in this extreme sacrifice of self-capitulation. Yet here the two figures part most sharply. The selflessness of her act well reflects Beate's heart, but such an unsparing exposure to the lover of everything ignoble in her own soul was something that Beate, with her modest and timid femininity, would have been incapable of. She would rather have sacrificially invented some evil she had not committed rather than expose, in that fashion, one act really committed. Only in Rebecca—in a Rebecca of an earlier unruly disposition—may the heroism of confession grow into a love stronger and greater than the modesty of love, so relentless that it could tear the inmost secret from the soul, naked and quiveringly exhibited, in order to save the other person's soul. One can observe that as soon as Rebecca loses her passivity and again acts, the difference between herself and Beate again emerges, despite Rebecca's change of mind.

During the momentary confusion, Rosmer, whose hopes and beliefs collapse after her confession, is incapable of valuing her act for its true worth. An insight into the past only confuses him. Consequently, Kroll's influence is renewed and he succeeds in having Rosmer drop all his liberated plans and ideas and rejoin his erstwhile friends. But precisely this situation causes Rosmer to feel even more deeply how his supposed strength, indeed his sentiment, is completely rooted in Rebecca; his dreamed-of freedom amounts to nothing more than dependence upon her.

For that reason, Rebecca's initial contempt and condemnation of Rosmer, after his return from Kroll and his friends, turn into desperation. He realizes that without belief in her, he would be rudderless; soon he asks, not only desperately but also yearningly, "How can I trust you fully and completely?" She does not remind him that in her self-sacrificing confession lies absolute proof of her change of mind. She is ready to do whatever he may wish in order to restore voluntarily and gladly his confidence in being able to affect people for the better. She knows that he also finds himself in the same painful and unbearable conflict; he is estranged from his former self and unable to allow his new self to translate itself into a full life.

As they converse sadly and affectionately, in doubt and desperation, there already is evident the mutual and sickly condition which they have brought upon themselves. And we are touched, as we would be by the fever-induced fantasies of a sick person, when Rosmer suddenly hits upon the idea that only one thing could restore his faith in Rebecca: her glad and voluntary death in the millstream. It touches us like a fevered hallucination when he pictures with seductive, inner horror how she would stand on the millstream dam, hesitant and shuddering, bending ever lower. With this brutal egoism, he reminds us of Rebecca herself as she wished for Beate's death; it seems that even her fantasy has taken hold of him. But this similarity is not unfounded; it does not only stem from their infecting each other, but is also based on the egoism of a maimed will. Egoism cannot exist without belief in others and their support, or be without the drive for self-preservation. It cannot exist in an unanchored and divided mind before which his real love for Rebecca momentarily retreats. Even the way he courts Rebecca tells of a persistent weakness of will. He wanted a new reality that would kill the past; a stronger will, first of all, would have built upon an already dead past and not have used love as a means of abusing a new life.

For Rebecca, however, it is only a slight sacrifice to die for Rosmer. For him and his peace of mind, she already has died a thousand times over when she devalued her life for his sake and exposed herself to his contempt. It was immaterial to her whether or not the waves would swamp her worthless and soul-emptied life. In Rebecca's quiet willingness lies the indifference of one who is deathly ill and contemplates her own demise, and whose will moreover has been broken through Rosmer's influence.

In view of her willingness to save her honor in his eyes, Rosmer's strange and feverish fantasy abandons him now. As he regains belief, love also breaks through—that love with which his wavering self is tied to her. How would he have been capable of being effective, in the least, without her? He can only follow her—be it even into death. It is quite noteworthy that in the moment of death their mutual love celebrates its full triumph and unites them forever; it is the moment when they realize their total inability to continue life, after they have debilitated, infected and weakened each other. Tightly embraced and mutually bound, they plunge into the waves as death appears to them only as the outer reflex of an already inwardly completed process. Rebecca is well aware that this conclusion does not spring from the clarity of a healthy and ineluctable decision, but that it represents the culmination of the sickness and confusion to which they finally succumb.

"What if all this were only a delusion," said Rebecca, "like one of these white horses at Rosmersholm?" And Rosmer agrees, "That could well be."

With justification then, the superstitions of Mrs. Helseth and those of the countryside have the last word: "The dead wife has fetched them."

The more it becomes evident that the infectious and debilitating love in their will and character is a dissolution of self, the more does that sickness gain force over their minds through superstitious horror. Even a clear awareness changes nothing of the inner necessity of such a course; no less does the sick person submit to his deadly plague, though he can distinguish his fever-fantasies from reality.

And so it happens that the strongest and most rash of all female figures ends like the tiniest and most childlike among them: in a death-sacrifice for another. There is one difference though. In Hedwig, both motives are combined, while they distribute themselves onto Rosmer and Rebecca: on the one hand, it is the devastating disillusionment with a supremely admired person; on the other hand, it is the wish to restore to that person his self-confidence and belief by offering a proof of love through her death. From the one Ibsen drama to the other, these thoughts intertwine. The contrast between Rebecca and Hedwig consists essentially in the fact that Rebecca's love is so exclusively dependent on Rosmer because she has lost her self, while Hedwig as a child had not as yet gained a mature independence. She dies because she has not *as yet* come into a life of her own; Rebecca dies because she *no longer* possesses a life of her own. Just as Hedwig's entire development rises and founders in her childhood, so Rebecca's blossoming into femininity overpowers her entire personality with all its earlier force.

In a significant way, Rebecca's death directly follows that of Ulric Brendel, her countryman from their homeland of the unrestrained and the obstinate. Both bleed to death because of the all-too-great losses suffered through the most innate gifts of life: he dies because of his powerless idealism, and she dies because of her ideal-less power. Brendel succumbs in battle and contention with an opponent; Rebecca succumbs through her tragic submission to her opponent. Brendel, as a man, kills himself because he has lost the flag to the enemy; Rebecca, as a woman, is conquered and sacrifices herself to the enemy because of her inner conflicts and her love for him. Both, however, atone for their wildness and unconstraints. Neither the superabundance of Brendel's ideals nor Rebecca's excess of strength saves either of them; just as she could not harness her powers to serve the ideal, so he did not know how to dominate life and reality through his treasures. He carelessly disperses and wastes the most precious seeds, instead of obtaining their fruit through patient work.

One would not wish for him to have the industriousness of a Kroll. If Kroll appears as a fanatic follower of tradition, who often is prejudiced and limited, he also is in the grip of a strong, unified view of the world that prompts enthusiastic, idealistic, and creative energy; his seedings take hold, so that ideals and reality come to organic fruition. That permits him to be sound as a bell and self-assured. In Kroll, as in Rosmer, both of whom are representatives of tradition, lies a power without which Brendel and Rebecca hopelessly shatter: that is the power of "education through the ideal."

While Brendel is wrecked, he gives involuntary testimony to the power of education through the ideal; Rebecca readily admits that in her freedom, an ideal moment had been missing, so that she was unable to pose something of her own against the ties that bind Rosmer to tradition. And so his ideals, which were completely alien to her being, made her sickly. She pays the price by pining and dying. When she takes that sickness upon herself and exchanges her soul, as strong as nature, for one which is tender and ennobled, she forever joins her world to that of Rosmer's. In turn, Rosmer is incapable of absorbing her free and nature-given strength and fusing the contrasts within himself; he then binds himself to Rebecca. Although they die because of their pact, and although death is the sole priest who may bless this pact of irreconcilables, Rosmer marries her: "Rebecca—here I place my hand upon your head and make you my legitimate wife!"

In this last picture, they point far beyond their own necessary tragedy and dissolution of personality. They nevertheless point to the fact that there must be a unity, a completion, a relatedness wherein a world with barriers and a world of freedom permeate each other and become reconciled. No more contention between them, no more enticements to pull one or the other into their respective camps, no victory; what remains only is an indistinguishable rooting in one another—a marriage.

It is Rebecca who feels things most wonderfully: submission

of self and self-preservation—these contradictory and destructive forces that have torn her inwardly—now have become mutually dependent and releasing; they are inseparably one.

"Is it you who follow me, or do I follow you?" she asks at death's threshold. "We will never get to the bottom of that question," answers Rosmer, "never will we be able to fathom that wonder." But, consoled, he embraces her because he knows that a solution has been found for the riddle of their lives, though it be a solution that finds release in death: "We go together, Rebecca . . . because now we two are one."

V   ELLIDA

>*"The transformation came when you*
>*let me choose freely."*

INFECTION, sickness and death are synonymous with attraction, love and betrothal in *Rosmersholm*. For behind these lurk the old contradictions between instinct and order, freedom and enslavement, the world of nature and the attic, except that they no longer give witness to their incompatibility through enmity and strife but through the tragedy of their harmony. More bitter, in fact, than the most lacerating battles which Nora or Mrs. Alving waged for emancipation is the discord within which self-sacrifice and downfall inevitably coincide.

At the same time that Rebecca chooses self-sacrifice and therefore her downfall, she forcibly joins seemingly disparate elements and readily pushes beyond mere contradictions in her loving and dying. Because her strength is sapped by love, she can no longer conquer and resolve those inward contradictions. She only points to the inevitability of a solution and prepares for it by sharpening the contradictions: she must suffer and die because of them. Still, suffering and death, quite naturally, complement and dignify her total being. During the course of Rebecca's sickness, it seemed that a crisis, new health and healing, and birth were taking shape. Only some remnant of youthful strength needed to assert itself; but her strength was spent and exhausted, necessarily allowing sickness to lead to death.

Infection, sickness and death: within these words Rebecca's life diminishes. But the pealing takes on a questioning sound and awaits an answer: Where is the new life which heals sickness and dying? Where is the physician who knows a remedy of which he can say, "Herein lies the strength for change"? Ellida, "The Lady from the Sea," attempts to answer the question. She comes from the sea, meaning that she emerges from the same origin as Rebecca. She comes from a region where an airy fullness of dimension and freedom reign in nature, where even in the soul of people there still exists an elemental rise and downward gliding, where nothing has ossified or is irrevocably bound to stony customs and traditions that hem in free motion, as do the mountains and valleys that close in upon the inhabitants of the fjords.

To such confinements, Ellida, like Rebecca, remains a stranger. Nora and Mrs. Alving lived in regions where boulders and nature's barriers broke strong-willed seawaves and caused them to find, and suit themselves to, new directions; such boulders and barriers ruggedly jutted into Nora's and Mrs. Alving's youth. Yet despite the narrowness of the valleys, they found paths toward the ideal peaks of life to which Ellida was a stranger indeed.

Although Ellida, aptly characterized as a pagan through her first name, grows up wild and unsupervised in the isolated light-tower at the sea, one point decisively distinguishes her life from Rebecca's chaotic upbringing: Ellida is spared the categorically damaging influences that prematurely and forcibly aroused violent instincts in Rebecca's being and which, in a sense, made her corruptively experienced. A deeper, more undisturbed purity hovers over Ellida, in contrast to the primitive innocence of Rebecca, who lived instinctively and untamed. Ellida still is naïve and inexperienced, and looks toward a personal ripening; but Rebecca already had ripened, specifically in a narrow direction which necessarily inhibited full inner growth. Superficially viewed, she seemed to have developed more fully than Ellida; but in essence she proves lacking in her capacity to develop, much like a noble creature of the wild which, in its self-sufficiency, is superior to a child, but which also appears inferior.

The difference between Rebecca and Ellida is distinctly significant because it sharpens and embosses a situation in which Ellida is a corrective to her predecessor: Ellida's development broadens and branches out into manifold possibilities. The reason why Rebecca's boundaries are not necessarily Ellida's is already predictable; moreover, Rebecca's experience and strength cannot help her to maneuver sufficiently to avoid breaking at the point of tragic insight, whereas at the same point of crisis a healing, growth and determination set in for Ellida.

The combination of Ellida's incapacity for change and her extreme youth makes it appear that she is helpless in the face of life. She has neither Rebecca's confident strength nor her brash assuredness that steers over waves and through storms toward happiness. Ellida is content to stand at the seashore and let her dreams glide over the waves which bode both terror and beauty, and whose depths cradle things marvelous and terrifying.

While the figure of Rebecca is challenging and spiteful, Ellida is full of expectancy and dreams. But her dreams remain much more formless than Rebecca's well-defined hopes. The waves that foam about Rebecca's imaginary ship in high seas awaken more definite wishes and fears than the wide, shimmering surfaces which Ellida views languidly, and which nowhere afford a resting place for eyes or thought, but instead form an infinite playroom for a roaming imagination that creates figments of fantasy. This strong development of a life of the imagination at the expense of a latent will to action is the second tendency that separates Ellida from Rebecca. An element of sickness—or predisposition to sickness—lies in that tendency, which can be conquered only by the full maturity of conscious will. Yet it contains a line that interiorizes and deepens her will, a situation which protects her from the kind of sudden, brutal spitefulness that possesses Rebecca. Within the silence of Ellida's soul, the gentlest and finest stirrings become articulate before unconscious drives become action. Once Ellida's will burgeons into a conscious and healthy force, it can achieve a much nobler and more refined adult articulation than Rebecca's. An opposite direction is taken by Rebecca; she starts from a point of vigorous but precocious activity, and then falls into a sickly paralysis when her total development lags behind a tardily awakened mature disposition.

Rebecca is vibrantly alive, though her maturity is impeded, while Ellida is unripe and given to fantasizing. Such differences of personality are mirrored distinctly again in the manner and destiny of their loves. While Rebecca's passion has a subjugating fatality about it, Ellida's persistent passivity invites a compulsive love, a daemonic compulsion of will which excludes free choice. While Rebecca strives to penetrate and ruthlessly analyze matters with full and clear judgment, Ellida succumbs to the charm of the unknown and the incomprehensible. During the course of her life, all persons near her, about whom she knew nothing definite, or did not wish to know more, exerted power over Ellida, especially the one who so characteristically remained the nameless stranger until the very end. It is the mysterious stranger's power which explains her love for him. It is the love of an immature creature who, with trepidation and a helpless will, faces a totally strange and deeply veiled, mysterious and unlit life; and yet, at the same time, Ellida is driven by the urgency of her fantasies to take the plunge. A yearning for submersion and the fear of it compete within Ellida; happiness and revulsion, attraction and threat co-exist. She loves him like a symbol become flesh incarnate, like life itself with its disguised freedom and force; it is as if she had looked into infinity, the limitless and the indeterminable. She seems to absorb his essence when she compares him with the elements of nature; he has the effect of a symbol. "That man," says Ellida, "is like the sea." Precisely because she lacks any personal assertiveness, his power grows limitless, becomes tenacious, and dominates her. From the start, her symbolization of his figure, and her identification of that mysterious figure with the strangeness of life, are deeply rooted in her nature and raise her relationship with him beyond the level of a simple affair of the heart. Here we see no single emotion or passion but an ethical problem related to the development of conscious will. Ellida only vaguely understands the semiconscious drives that urge on toward life; her imagination dominates her and personifies those drives through the daemonic grip of the strange man. A contrast becomes sharply evident, particularly when one compares the shifting and illusory symbol represented by the stranger with Rebecca's passion for Rosmer, which is so completely rooted in sensual reality. Then one understands why Rebecca's love must disintegrate and die, reflecting the disintegration and demise of her strong personality and being. On the contrary, Ellida is able to shake off the stranger's compelling force because of her own development and experience. We find here the difference between dream and life, symbol and person.

With sensitive verisimilitude, Ibsen brings into conjunction the realistic appearance of the stranger and Ellida's symbolic, fantasized conception of him. In every detail—even the smallest—the stranger appears in different colorations, depending upon the sober or dreamlike spotlight cast upon him. He is as iridescent as the seawaves, depending upon whether they are struck by the light of the day or the moon. Without doubt he appears as an experienced, adroit and fearless adventurer who has coped as thoroughly with life as with the turbulence of the sea. The untamed and stormy independence of the sea is an element in which he can breathe most freely. To Ellida it appears that he arises from the waves onto that lonely beach. His past remains remote and alien to her, as if it rested in the depths of the sea. Nothing serves to enlighten her about his personality. And, quite consistently, nothing in the darkness of their brief and secretive conversations illuminates his being. Not even is there talk about his seafaring. Their talk is only about the sea itself and its breakers, about the calmed sea and the dangers of storms, of clear nights and the midday sun pouring upon the isolated stretches where the sea lions and the dolphins slumber motionless. He talks to her about things which they both know and love: the reality which he has learned about firsthand from experience with the surf, which for her, at the beach, was a matter of symbolic longing. Slowly his physiognomy disappears so completely behind these visualizations that it seems to Ellida as if both she and he—like relatives—belong together with all the creatures of the sea.

And just as his manner of speaking supports her fantasized conception of the man, so does his manner of action: he acts forcefully, determinedly, as witnessed by the murder of the captain and by his adventurous engagement to Ellida at the seashore; and yet, he is silent, mysterious and abrupt—one need think only of the quick and silent motions of the fish beneath the surface, which one can only indistinctly follow. At no time whatever do we see the motives that prompt him; they remain impenetrable and unintelligible. In all, here are tendencies which distinctly characterize his adventuresome appearance on the scene, which so mysteriously mates itself to Ellida's sickly life of the imagination.

The influence he exerts upon her grows in proportion to the revulsion he imparts to her. When he joins Ellida to him eternally through the engagement at the seashore—as with an act of magic—and later flees from the scene where he committed a murder and sinks back into the waves from which he had arisen, Ellida heaves a sigh of relief. She makes the decision to take back her word by means of a letter. But he disregards her decision and claims her as his possession. The recalling of her promise and the attempt at freeing herself remain gestures as helpless as those of a child who throws a rock at the sea in order to restrain the floods from plundering the shore. The stranger has the same persistent, rapacious ruthlessness with which passion seizes what it desires, without inclination, like the sea, to return its booty. Something of this stormy cold-bloodedness of the sea seems to lie in the stranger's faithfulness to his intentions, a clinging to elemental necessity that takes no account of the sensitivities of another being. The stranger's cold-bloodedness, despite his long-preserved faithfulness, also explains the surprising manner with which he gives up Ellida at the end of the drama, without lament or threat: "Goodby, then, Mrs. Wangel! From now on, you are nothing more in my life than a shipwreck which I have survived."

No storm is raised by the sea when its booty has eluded it; it continues its motions placidly. When, however, the same stranger, whose loss of Ellida seemed to have left him untouched, is threatened by Dr. Wangel with loss of his freedom and imprisonment, he immediately draws his pistol and is resolutely determined to commit suicide. In no instance does he act with more sober calculation than here, but at the same time, nowhere except during his last appearance is there a fantastic and effective illumination. His sudden yielding up of Ellida reminds one of an abrupt retreat by the evil power of a ghost when confronted by a magic formula. His words re-enforce this feeling: "I see it now. Here is something stronger than my will."

The impression created by that scene is marvellously consonant with the mood of the play's closing in the setting of a summer's midnight. Neither the light of the moon nor the stars, but instead the common light of the sunset in the middle of the night magically contributes to a fairytale clarity. The inner spiritual life of each character is driven to the limit of tension, so that words and actions separate themselves like involuntary incantations and have the powerful impact of magic. Yet, in fact, each person's words and actions are the result of a slow and necessary development for which the characters are prepared. Ultimately, the symbolic and the fantastic are nourished exclusively by strongly interrelated psychological events and problems. No less does this apply to Ellida than to her conception of the stranger. No less does this explain her sudden transformation than his sudden renunciation. Since the stranger only represents for Ellida her own imperfect understanding of what she wants from life, it only takes a final maturity of will to break his power and let him sink into nothingness. The drama of this happening is predicated on the stranger's power to exert—even from a distance—his influence upon her up to the decisive moment. Because the stranger's personality is of lesser importance than her inner conceptualizations of him, no distance really separates them; at any hour the man can overwhelm her with his daemonic power. His power lay not in his disregard of Ellida's attempt to withdraw her engagement promise and free herself, but rather in the fact that at the time she was still incapable of inwardly freeing herself from him and pitting a mature, fully developed will against his.

So it is that Ellida's development takes on the shape of a love conflict which could be entitled "The Return of the Stranger" or "The Vengeance of the Stranger." Does it not suggest similar titles for *Rosmersholm*, "Vengeance" or "Beate's Return"? In both cases, isn't it a ghostly superpower that rises from the waves and transcends separation and death? In fact, many interchangeable relationships inform both dramatic compositions. In highly characteristic fashion for Ibsen, circumstances remain similar; only the persons have been interchanged. In *The Lady from the Sea*, it's not Beate's shadow—a spirit of helpless love and self-sacrifice that wanders about vengefully after it had to yield to the brutality of power—but an elemental power itself which grasps after its victim and which stretches out its ghostly hand in an attempt to prevent the victim from exploiting a newly-won strength of independence. Accordingly, the outcomes are different: Beate dies and draws down with her the triumphant, coarse crime which, despite her weakness, she transcends through her spiritual transformation and ennoblement; so two avenging ghosts—Beate and the crime—weaken and destroy Rebecca. The stranger, however, must retreat before Ellida's spiritualized development because his crude and elemental power could only influence an unfocused life-seeking drive of an immature will.

The disparateness of the solutions occurs in that Rebecca reminds one of the stranger, while one feature in Beate's makeup suggests a similar one in Ellida, namely, the sensitivity of her soul which harbors the potential seeds for a deeper ripening. Certainly, it is this one feature (Beate is thoroughly rooted in the traditional) which is exclusively found in the confines of an ivory-tower world. But Ellida strives for the wider reaches of freedom. For that reason, opposite causes bring them sorrow and sickness: Beate's limited world is brought to ruin by Rebecca's wild energy; Ellida's inner life becomes sickly when she is hemmed in by the oppressiveness of a narrow world. When this occurs through marriage to Dr. Wangel, it also triggers an inner battle which again conjures up the stranger. She had imagined that she could escape the stranger's grasp completely if, in her distress, she would seize Dr. Wangel's hand and follow him as his wife into a family life. But the opposite took place. The more she attempts to escape her past, in fact through the seclusion of her new life, all the more do her old fantasies assume a reality. The new and comforting family situation plunges her into an oppressive, claustrophobic mood, which is re-enforced by her surroundings—high crags and mountains—that everywhere project strict, immovable barriers and boundaries. Since the waters of the fjords move sluggishly in the absence of the great flow of ebb and tide and their foaming freshness, Ellida too yearns for the greater vistas of life. From the lonely seashore where she has betrothed herself forever to the stranger, the unknown distances stretch far. If, with an involuntary shudder, she experienced the stranger's daemonic power at that time in the form of an overwhelming compulsion, so she now thinks only of the limitless freedom into which the stranger wanted to force her. If earlier she felt enticed by a magic force to hurl herself into the sea—blindly, with outstretched arms, and against her will—now it seems to her as if the stranger wanted to reveal to her all the magnificence of the sea's depths. The unknown aspects of life from which she felt herself forever separated remained vague and seductive like the sea whose roaring and whispering echoed in all her thoughts and dreams. This frame of mind rendered her oblivious to the voices of reality around her, and only escalated the sickly one-sidedness of her fantasies and passive expectations.

A change of her disposition could not be effected by Wangel, who amiably tolerates her whims and moods as if she were a child. Somewhat similarly, the stranger also treated her like a dependent and immature child. Yet, she felt intensely the contrast between the husband and the lover. The latter controlled her unpracticed will and forced her submission to his, and under the daemonic compulsion of his dominion, he drew her irresistibly onto high seas, the foaming vastness of life. Her husband, on the contrary, envelops her with considerateness and pampering, preserves her from influences which could change her, and relieves her of any work, tasks and responsibilities; at the same time he chains her to the pitiful narrowness of his existence, within which she despairs of being able to move freely. In effect, he condemns her to the restless pacing of a prisoner who has formerly been accustomed to freedom, and so—without intending it— he becomes a guilty party to her estrangement from him. Originally, her love was directed toward Wangel, pushing away the memory of the stranger. "I have completely forgotten him," she confessed. What again conjured up the stranger had nothing to do with any change in her inclinations, because in the same breath she says to Wangel, "I love no one except you."

Yet beyond all inclinations, impulse and yearning prompt Ellida, who has been enlightened by no one about life, nor given any stake or task in it. Wangel could only lessen her demand for the presence of the unknown stranger when he acquainted her with a small slice of life wherein love and activity could be purposeful. That is what Ellida would have needed most instinctively because she later reproaches Wangel for not having exerted greater determination to ensconce her in his world: "I am so completely without roots in your house, Wangel. The children are not my own . . . If I go away tonight . . . I have no key to give up nor any instructions to leave behind. From the very beginning, I have been far outside of everything."

Just as people around Ellida are unable to break her passivity, so is she incapable of jealousy toward Wangel's deceased wife who has remained dear in his memory and that of the children. Already in the first scene, when Ellida appears, we see elaborate floral arrangements being made to secretly commemorate the dead mother. Honest and gentle in all things, Ellida acknowledges the propriety of these remembrances all the more as she herself lives in the past. Quite readily one compares the neat flower scene with the voluptuous weight of flowers with which Rebecca freights every room in Rosmersholm so that their sweet fragrance would help Rosmer to forget the dead, who cannot tolerate joys and flowers. How gently Ellida's behavior differs from that of the passionate self-serving of Rebecca is clear when she graciously adds her flowers to the big bouquet of the children's flowers: "Shouldn't I join the birthday party for . . . mother?" It is precisely the more passive and gentle character of Ellida that finds expression equally through kindness or indifference that causes a seeming paradox, namely that the impressionable Ellida remains uninfluenced by her surroundings much longer than Rebecca. From the very start, Rebecca takes charge of all things and people—whether alive or dead—at Rosmersholm; she invests such faithful energy in these pursuits that later she is unable to muster enough willpower to escape from the inner circle. The manner of existence at Rosmersholm is completely contagious; the infection thrives on intimate and strong relationships.

The fact that Ellida and Wangel do not lose their individualities through mutual contact permits a later flowering of a much healthier relationship. Ultimately, Ellida's innermost marriage to Wangel becomes an independent, voluntary act and conscious choice. Different is Rebecca's self-assertion: only in death can she marry her lover. Instead of the wild energy and the sickliness which combine in a deadly fashion to constrict Rebecca and Rosmer, there reigns in Wangel, as well as in Ellida, a sensitivity sufficiently alert to permit enough room for the needs of the other to find an outlet. Instead of an irresistible attraction for the opposite, there grows quite slowly—despite misunderstandings and estrangements—a tranquil and sure attraction born of the hidden affinities of their souls. This early became evident when Ellida intuitively sought the companionship of her husband. The first words which we hear from her lips express not a yearning for the sea and the far-away but for Wangel's return, as if she could not bear to be without him even for an hour: "Is it you, Wangel? Thank God, you've come back." Despite her passionate urge for the stranger, she is driven toward Wangel, seeking his embrace: "My dearest . . . save me from that man!" She has the feeling that Wangel will protect her: "I'll find peace and a harbor if

I could only come very close to you and try to resist all those tempting and awful powers." In the next breath she adds, "But that, I don't dare . . . I can't do it!" The stranger elicits from her a *compulsion* to love, but her *desire* for love is directed toward her husband. The faintness of her will bonds her to the stranger, but Ellida's intuition secretly suggests that Wangel will assist her in finding herself as a person. "Oh, Wangel, help me! Save me!" Ibsen has so delineated Wangel that his relationship to Ellida can be understood in those terms. Like the other major figures of the drama, Wangel possesses a spiritual physiognomy with a double perspective: he seems to hark back to *Rosmersholm,* but also has the faculty of looking ahead toward a new and happier life. Just as specific features of Ellida remind one of Beate, and Rebecca's remind one of the stranger, so Wangel resembles Rosmer, but transcends him by far.

Piety in Rosmer's existence played much too great a role. Wangel too cannot free himself from his dead wife, although he found a successor to her. He did not even have the strength to forbid the children's secretiveness, which apparently derived from a sense of piety toward the first mother. Just as Rosmer in his outward life and actions is bound to be influenced, by the dead and the weight of the past, so Wangel too clings to the accustomed and seems not to know how to gain a vigorous, independent way of life. His daughter Bolette complains that "Papa never gets anything done," and he agrees. The tendency toward piety causes a laming of his will. In the face of situations which require redoubled efforts for solution, he is often incapable of pulling himself together. When he marries Ellida, it is less from an urge toward a renewed life or love than an attempt to find through affection a way to escape the pain of loneliness and the ties of his old love; and, when his new marriage is profoundly shaken, he occasionally anaesthetizes his sorrow through the pleasure of wine.

But given even these habits, Dr. Wangel is significantly different from Rosmer. Above all, he is not a spiritual captive of his heredity nor of any personal weakness; he recognizes his deficiencies with misgivings, and his insights lead to a clearer view of open vistas ahead. Unlike Rosmer, he is not helplessly under the influence of the loved one; he feels a responsibility to watch over her, and reproaches himself for having done so in a mindless and selfishly pampering manner: "I should have been like a father to her—and, at the same time, a guide! I should have done everything possible to develop her mind and to teach her to think clearly." And his piety toward his deceased wife is not grounded, as it is with Rosmer, in a stolid obligation to carry a corpse on his back throughout life. No, it is a surviving intimacy of feeling, a warmly preserved faithfulness whose steadfastness must also be acknowledged as genuine by the living. It is the same faithfulness which he later extends to Ellida, with a patient display of self-sacrifice. On the one hand, this relates Wangel to Rosmer, but on the other, he is more of a rationally selfless being with the capacity to develop. Wangel does not permit himself to be passively destroyed by another person. Within him is a strength of love that allows him to empathize with others and help them; he possesses insight and reason. Because his ability to love is rooted in such positive strength, it remains truly selfless; while Rosmer's seeming selflessness or weakness of will turns into a self-seeking direction at the moment of crisis, so that he demands Rebecca's death to gain manliness and effectiveness in his own life. In stark contrast, Wangel willingly gives Ellida her freedom at the end of the drama. His personal hopes and wishes retreat more and more as his deep instincts to help and to heal assert themselves.

Their different professions emphatically distinguish Rosmer and Wangel. Rosmer was a preacher, and therefore a representative of traditional ethics to which he submitted his own will and from which he could not free himself without going under and without inviting an inner conflict. As a doctor, Wangel must comprehend and be able to detect the source of his patients' pain, but as a professional he must avoid contracting their illness or becoming infected. He must seek to heal, but understand his limitations. It is significant, though, that only when he is faced with sickness is he forced to draw upon his best resources, a challenge without which he would not have escaped the influence of a conventional life. For Ellida, too, he has superficial inclinations at first. When she becomes sick, however, he becomes a self-sacrificing and understanding doctor of the soul. Her suffering ripens his love to the point of selfless intimacy and joyful, devoted attention. One can say that through her feverish fantasies, he first forms a clear conception of her total being and he takes a true measure of the honest and painfully yearning sound of her voice. Earlier, when she was well, he was incapable of giving her the love and guidance that would have allowed her to avoid the dangers that attend her maturing. For that he would have had to be not only a devoted doctor but also, in the highest sense, a spiritual guide who knows how to interpret the inner life and how to exorcise the appalling and mysterious lure of the unknown and boundless. Only a spiritual guide can teach one how to recognize the definite tasks set by life and their deepest significance.

Wangel's own development is incomplete; he is still in need of fulfillment. And yet, his deepest love for Ellida comes about as he senses in Ellida's estranging fantasies those elements which he lacks. He still lives in an ivory tower, but already his will—a drive toward freedom—stirs powerfully; "There is a pounding of the surf, an ebb and flow, in her thoughts and in her feelings," says Wangel in comparing Ellida with the sea. Then he voices the reason for his being drawn to her irresistibly: "You are a kin of the sea . . . and the terrifying, Ellida. That attraction is the strongest part of you." And one can easily grasp how much these mutual needs for fulfillment contribute to Wangel's efforts to give Ellida a "true marriage," a complete merger of beings, as soon as he is able to encourage in her the same honest self-understanding which he possesses.

Wangel succeeds, step by step, in moving from external appearances and the surface of life into the inner depths and source of strength which he transforms into an external and liberating force. Ellida's path to the external is blocked, and she sickens in the depth of her inwardness, where she is limited to a life of fantasy. Slowly, however, a changing mood effects a positive substitution of the outer for the inner life. Through the force of her imagination, her past assumes a new reality and momentarily penetrates into the present. "You think and feel by means of images—and through visualizations," Wangel tells her. (Artistically these factors relate *The Lady from the Sea* to Ibsen's other dramas, each, as it were, being a last act that climactically sums up implicit and long internal developments off stage. Ellida's madness conjures up the past in all its richness and brings it into

the light of day with sharper relief than Rebecca's pangs of conscience and Mrs. Alving's reflections succeed in doing. The last
two figures only narrate, while Ellida at the same time aestheti-
cizes her memories.)

What Ellida vividly sees in her thoughts is real to her; what, at
the moment, she cannot precisely actualize, *that* is suddenly lost
as if it had died. When this happens in her relationship with
Wangel, she cannot find him, nor can she find it in her to be a wife
to him; and that becomes "so terribly tormenting." Even if the
stranger appears vividly only in her mind, she succumbs to his
presence as if it were real, and she is gripped by terror. He does
not appear to her as does a loved one who through lifelike
memory (or even through hallucination) is called up by a hopeless yearning. No, it is the uncanny actuality of his presence that
becomes so tormenting to Ellida, and as soon as she can firmly
convince herself of his absence, she calms down. So it is not her
feelings or needs which the stranger provokes, but her will that
becomes lame and overwhelmed when she thinks about him. It
seems to her that he seizes her with unbelievable, ghostly power
and forcibly betroths himself anew. Also, when he appears to her
in her imagination, he does so without casting an eye upon her,
so to speak, and without her really wanting to see him in any
particulars. He even stands "a bit to the side; he never looks at
me. He simply *is* there."

This way of viewing is extraordinarily true in Ibsen's delinea-
tion and is analogous to vivid dream images. These consist of a
certain diffuseness and general vagueness, coupled with extreme
clarity and precision in some details. So, for instance, in Ellida's
memory the actual externals of the stranger had become so
blurred that she does not recognize him again when he shows up
in Wangel's garden. On the other hand, in the images of her
fantasy, she clearly sees the blue-white pearl in his tiepin, and the
"dead fish eye" which symbolizes everything that gruesomely
relates to her visions. As soon as the general fuzziness lifts and
the stranger stands before Ellida and Wangel, the effect of the
dream vision becomes more diluted.

For that reason, Wangel greets the return of the stranger as a
happy turn for the better: "Now you have a new and truer image
of him in your mind. And that overshadows the old one, so that

you can't see it any longer . . . And it overshadows your sick imaginings too. That's why it is good that reality finally has come."

The stranger's return is a necessary requirement for Ellida's healing and her inner release from him. Naturally, the second requirement is the return of her husband into her heart and mind. In contrast to the strange man, Wangel is constantly near her, but he is held at a distance by the symbolic dream image of the stranger in her interior life. She takes no notice of Wangel's deep attachment to her; it steadily swells into a powerful love which finally succeeds in wresting her from the stranger. Instinctively she turns to her husband, but only as would a sick patient turn to her doctor who might possibly bring relief from pain. She still does not know that his only healing power lies in his capacity for love. Ellida's understanding of Wangel was made more difficult by his necessarily gradual maturation and his slow reaching out to her. Further, only isolated and decisive images of the moment made an impact upon her fantasies; these images were interiorized and given sharp and somber elaboration in the aura of growing fantasy. She was too sickly to notice attentively any long-range developments.

With that, her relationship to Wangel appears to her only in the same light in which it had originally commenced; an engagement that took place only after a slight acquaintance and the existence of a mutual affection, enhanced on both sides by motives which had nothing to do with love. She only remembers how lonely she felt and how she was not understood by people in Wangel's household; but at no time did she pay attention to the tender efforts of Wangel to understand her better. His words attest to that: "I am beginning to understood you— slowly . . . Years of living together have made me more aware."

Because she lacks perception of what goes on about her, Ellida attributes no great sacrifice to Wangel if he were to set her free when she finally requests that he "cancel the original transaction." And Wangel, with selfless goodness, feels that in certain respects he owes her that sacrifice, even if she is not capable of doing it honor. Actually, he had missed the opportunity to redirect, in time, Ellida's emotional disturbance onto free and healthy soil where she could have taken root and become integrated with his world. Now as she struggles, with increasing inner violence, to tear herself free from him, Wangel does not wish to incur the guilt of seeing her bleed away in her drive toward a dreamed-for freedom. He knows that her passion for the stranger is nothing more than an urge toward freedom. "Your longing for the sea and thinking about it—your wish to follow him, that strange man," Wangel says to her later, "that was the expression of an awakening and growing inner demand for freedom. Nothing more."

However, because she feels that he does not understand her and is a stranger to her inner emotions, she regards her marriage as an involuntary imprisonment. Understanding and love make the difference between a bond which closely unites people to one another and a chain which forges them together. And in one single moment it is possible for a bond to become a chain, or the reverse. Ellida discovers this with surprise when she realizes that Wangel's love prompts him to set her free even to follow the stranger. Quiet and trembling, Ellida manages to say to Wangel, "Have I then come so close, so truly close to you!"

At that Wangel brings himself to release Ellida and to put the choice to her in order to preserve her from madness; he is in fact convinced that he has lost her. His sacrifice is meant seriously. But, without realizing it, he tears the blindfolds of delusion from her eyes. From the moment when she understands the dimension and intensity of his love, she no longer feels alien. She knows herself to be close to him and to be surrounded by a home rather than a prison atmosphere. If she had not been imprisoned, the drive to free herself would not have been meaningful. Freedom ceases to be tempting when it no longer is unattainable; Ellida stands on free soil.

It is easy to misunderstand her words, "I could have looked into the heart of the matter and could have entered it—if I had decided to do so. I could have chosen the unknown. And so, I could have rejected it as well." These words do not represent a whimsical smugness stemming from her transformation. She actually means to say: I no longer need freedom because I have understood that I am free. With that she no longer understands the free choice which Wangel has conceded to her. Indeed, only a day earlier she was ready to believe that losing her would affect

Wangel very little; she was sure, at the time, that she would follow the stranger. Given the freedom to make a choice, she now realizes that she no longer has a choice because the offer itself is an act of love. Earlier, her mental reconstruction of her engagement to Wangel has had a powerful, transforming effect upon her. Now that he is ready to give her up, another transformation occurs. Through apparent revelation she sees that Wangel is willing to go to any length—including deep self-laceration—in order to restore her to health and to heal her wounds. As if awakening from a frightening dream, she recognizes for the first time what he is really like. With that she celebrates his return into her heart after a long estrangement, while the stranger leaves it because reality finally has changed her image of him.

Although Wangel's act of love gives Ellida a feeling of freedom in his presence, it insufficiently explains her restoration to health; it only induces a crisis that will run its course successfully. True, the manic feeling that she is imprisoned has disappeared, but the root cause of the mania has not. To be accurate, Ellida was not forced to be a prisoner: rather she was a voluntary captive of the sickly, exaggerated and unfettered condition of her fantasy world and sought freedom through the limitless and the unknown. The cause lay in her hypnotic staring into the limitless, which was unintentionally furthered by Wangel's considerateness and pampering, and by a total lack of diverting duties and responsibilities. Basically then, Ellida suffered, like Rebecca, from an abuse of freedom and from an unchecked aimlessness of being, which necessarily produce an inner imagination synonymous with madness and mental derangement; Rebecca's instincts, too, trigger destructive actions and lame her will power. One small scene during the previous day clearly shows how Ellida progressively realizes that her deepest suffering stems from a withdrawal wherein she has lost herself in fruitless brooding and dreams. When Ellida is taken by surprise at the stormy affection shown her by the youngest stepdaughter, Hilde, and she is reprimanded by Hilde's sister Bolette for never reciprocating shy and concealed love, Ellida stops short, and asks doubtingly, "Ah! . . . Could there ever be a place for me in this home?" She senses an answer and possible rescue; her sickly line of thought is suddenly blocked by a totally new conception. She

senses that the daemonic compulsion which lures her into the
infinite and limitless could be rendered helpless by a will securely
anchored in self-imposed limitations, natural boundaries of
creativity and love.

In all, it is highly characteristic of Ellida that soon after her
return to her husband and in the midst of her new happiness, she
reaches out for responsible tasks and duties. When her spiritual
strength surges, she turns away from her debilitations and turns
her thoughts to other people. When Wangel calls out, "Oh—to
think that now we can live for each other," Ellida rapidly adds,
"And for both our children . . . who don't belong to me . . . but
I will win them over!" She now understands that she cannot be
truly at home in the isolation of her limitless dreamings and
yearnings but can find room in the narrowness of human relationships that allow full play for activity and love:

> Home is a place with room for five,
> but too narrow for two who are enemies.
> Home is where all your thoughts roam freely,
> where your voice reaches all hearts,
> and answers resound in familial tones.*

The second saving thought expressed by Wangel verbalizes Ellida's own, and it gives evidence of her freedom as well as her
personal sense of duty: "Now you may choose freely. The responsibility is yours, Ellida." She clasps her head and looks
toward Wangel, "A free choice . . . with responsibilities? Also
responsibilities? Here lies a possibility for change!" Free action
and personal responsibility mark Ellida's recovery and turn
toward reality . . . Those prerequisites allow a Nora to be free
and, on the other hand, allow the complete self-containment of
an Ellida.

If we follow Ellida's thoughts to their logical conclusion, we
find the unavoidable gaps in Nora's development. Nora cannot
permit herself to be restrained by incumbent obligations because
she has not reached the point of being able to accept them voluntarily. At the moment when Nora leaves us, she stands on the
threshold of her development and begins the uncertain ascent.

---

*From Ibsen's *Love's Comedy*, written previous to *Rosmersholm* and *The
Lady from the Sea* and which prefigures both in several ways.

She still does not know what her small world will look like from a different vantage point, nor how her personal life might be judged by a mature outlook. So Nora concludes with a mute question, while Ellida gives us the answer to why one woman sought to avoid home and responsibilities and the other sought to embrace them. It is therefore no coincidence that these two female figures possess similar traits, although their goals seem to lie in opposite directions. If one views Nora and Ellida side by side, one notices immediately that both have identical, immature figurations: Nora's narrow surroundings have not allowed her to attain an upright posture, while Ellida's posture has not attained a natural poise because nowhere on the wide seascape has she found anything against which to measure herself at full height. Nora seems stunted because her life in a doll's house has artificially sealed her off from life outside, and Ellida lacks stature because her dreamlike gaze dissolves reality into nebulous pictures.

Such deficiencies in the lives of Nora and Ellida invite catastrophes that lead to the decisive moments at the end of the plays. One also notices a similarity of conflicts, for in both instances the dramas deal with a battle between marital duties and personal freedom. Yes, superficially viewed, Ellida's situation contains a much more convincing motivation for *Nora's* separation from her husband, while in Nora's life there is much which eventually would make it easier for *Ellida* to return home to Wangel. This is true also of the relationships both to their husbands as well as to their children. The "Lady from the Sea" no longer has a child of her own, and the two stepdaughters will soon leave her care. For Nora, on the other hand, separation from her children is made possible through the coincidence that her own, old governess will remain with them and provide essential care.

Is not Nora's own neglected upbringing to be blamed for not having given her the guidance of a mother rather than of a governess? And must not this fault be repeated in the lives of the children? Not for the sake of liberty does Nora wish to free herself, but only for the purpose of discovering her full resources that would enable her to assume responsibilities and duties; she found it sinful to have become a wife, and indeed a mother, before she became a fully conscious human being in possession of herself. But is it possible to undo this blasphemy? Can she extinguish the children and their unique existence just as she is capable of extinguishing her marriage? Such questions Nora does not answer because she has no answer; she leaves the home in order to find an answer.

Superficially we also find a correspondence to this in Nora's relationship with Helmer. Seemingly, Ellida's reproach to Wangel is on a more solid footing. After all, he has removed her from an environment which has made her happy, and he has separated her from her home at the sea, knowing full well that transplanting her to a restrictive plot of land would do her damage. He feels that the damage could be made good only through her willing development under his guidance, and yet he leaves her to her own devices much too long. Helmer, by way of contrast, takes Nora as he finds her; he makes every effort to duplicate in detail the playroom of her father's house. Of her urge for inner freedom and greater dignity, he has not the slightest inkling because her childish behavior hides that urge completely. At any rate, Helmer is totally ignorant about Nora, for his love is egotistic and limited, a love without understanding and the spirit of sacrifice; but his deficiencies allow insight into the way he handles situations.

So one can note how thoroughly and inwardly Ibsen formulates psychic problems. If it is possible for Ellida to remain with her husband, there must be a minimal "necessary something" which would allow a full flowering and an effective enlargement of the sphere of love. If, on the other side, that "something" is missing, it becomes possible for Nora to stride ruthlessly forward—ignoring every obligation, love, children and husband—with only one goal in her sight.

Ibsen does not permit secondary motives to weaken the primary and strictly organic one. Well then, what is this one "something" which is the necessary foundation of a "true marriage"? It is truth and freedom. In Nora's case it would mean the possibility of developing from a doll to a full-bodied human being while living with Helmer. And for him, it would become necessary to reveal his love and lend it truth during the moment of testing and danger. Both these conditions are met in the marriage of Ellida and Wangel: she returns to him because he proves to her that no longer is she a prisoner in his house, but that she is free through the gift of sacrifice, a love which speaks graciously and selflessly, with convincing truthfulness.

In that sense, Nora's expectations are realized in Ellida's life: through Wangel's action, Nora's dream about "the most wonderful thing of all" has become a reality.

The very onset of the dream harbored the seeds of the drama's resolution; beginning and end lock together perfectly. For Nora, the dream had an emancipating strength which propelled her into independence and the single life, and which dissolved her home and marriage. The dream has become a reality. At the same time, the dream has become a unifying and binding force that newly constructs Ellida's home and marriage, which then pose a firm barrier to the urge for detachment and independence.

The longing for self-realization stems from the truthfulness of Nora's love: she wishes only to gain possession of herself so that she can offer that self as a gift. From her radiant inner health, a stream of joyous love is ready to spill over onto her husband and be transformed into a dream: the wonder of a true marriage. As for Ellida, her restlessness and the consuming fever of a sickly disposition drive her out of the family circle into a vague and substanceless freedom. The differing concepts of what is freedom could not be accented more sharply. In Nora's phrase about "the most wonderful thing of all" lies a naïve and devotional hope; in Ellida's notion of "the terrifying" lies the apprehensive gaze into an empty distance, attractive and repulsive, in which lies chaos and vacillation. Nora carries within herself the positive ideal of her love and will, while Ellida is at the mercy of an overwrought fantasy.

To the extent that Nora's emancipation represents not a personal whim but an ideal, the barriers which she had to surmount and the shackles she had to discard seemed to be undignified restraints. Nearly the opposite is true of Ellida. The world of the attic or the ivory tower with its constancy of order and confinement meant an empty doll's house and prison for Nora; for Ellida, they offer the means for learning and shelter. Rebecca was inextricably caught in a world capable of taming wildlife and polishing raw material, but she was taught to know freedom only by its opposite. Ellida is the one to experience the wonder of an expansive love that shatters the walls of the attic and admits powerful draughts of freedom and truth. She stands in a world that is protective, a place of unity and conciliation.

While Nora dreams her dream of the "wonderful," her thoughts circle indescribably high over the mean and dark earth. . . . For Ellida, "wonder" has become reality and nature; summer, like ivy, climbs all over Ellida's house and shades her greening secret. Ellida's face is suffused with the bridelike anticipation of a Nora, a wonder realized in the fullness of nature. "Don't you find," Hilde asked the knowledgeable friend of the family, Ballested, "that she and Papa look as if they have just gotten engaged?" And he answered, "It is summertime, little lady!" It is the summertime of a love that entrenches itself in a home and is surrounded by the full stream of life.

VI   HEDDA

"I stand here idly and shoot into the blue sky."

I N NONE of the early Ibsen dramas does the content of a work seem to concentrate so exclusively and exhaustively upon a central female figure as in *The Lady from the Sea*. While the minor figures only stir interest and achieve a life of their own in relation to a main figure, here they form a group of people standing in sharp relief from Ellida—who at the same time is in their midst— and demanding individualistic attention. They impress us as participants in a side-drama within the main drama; but although they embody no new problems that depart from the Ellida-theme in *The Lady from the Sea*, they are a series of diverse types in whom the same basic idea is mirrored. And the significance of the idea consists of its gliding over into other personalities and promoting the expansion of the problem, while Ellida's figure becomes the culmination of a long line of development. Yet in all this, the same basic rhythm resounds like the waves of the sea that roll against the banks with a steady beat, lifted out of the sea by a great, scalding billow that burrows out of the depths and foams with playfully curling white-caps. Despite the independence of the single life-portraits, a marvelous unity of mood still dominates, allowing one to sense the spiritual connections of the whole.

This unity of mood is all the more artistic as the feverish restlessness of the morbid expresses itself through her in an agitated dreaming that pulses into the unknown. This expresses itself masterfully through the purely external. Not only does Ellida's morbidity evidence itself in continual unrest and motion, but all those in Wangel's house also seem to find themselves in a state of incessant back-and-forth, aimless wanderings, in search for self and expression. And if we look closer at the local background against which this restlessness plays itself out, we notice an obvious overlay of inner and outer circumstances.

A small, confining fjord-city up north is revealed, in which for a long time the inhabitants lived isolated from the world's commerce and intellectual currents, like the "ancient crucian carp" in the pond of Wangel's garden. Annually, during the summer months, a stream of strangers winds its way through the small city and up to the marvels under the midnight sun. But that stream only goes through and does not rest there, nor does it take with it any of the crucians to join the wild shoal coming and migrating in nature. In the wake of that stream of strangers is an awakened fantasy, restlessly and vainly demanding an air of freedom, without however effecting any change in the reality of things.

"Sometimes I fear," said Ballested, "that our city will lose her old ways because of all the strange influx." And his own person testifies to that fear: instead of the prescribed efficiency of work associated with a shoal of fish, an entirely new, human way of thinking makes its appearance. He is quite "many-sided," for one must know how to acclimatize oneself in differing ways to small locales. Therefore he is, at one and the same time, a painter, decorator, barber and hair stylist, dancing instructor, a knowing guide for tourists, and chairman of the "Society for Horn-music." The "acclimatizing" in all this clearly is the opposite of a free and broad development and is only an arbitrary distortion of it.

Just as that foreign word "acclimatize" always comes stutteringly from his lips, so he also cannot move freely among his all-too-many occupations nor feel at home in them; he must force himself to pursue them, and unites them more in his fancy than in fact.

While Ballested's restlessness seeks practical outlets, we find the young Lyngstrand, the future sculptor, to be another type. He has no sense for the practical side of life. He flees from the confusion of excessive choices because they cannot aid in his creation of a masterpiece. He is vain, great plans hover before him, and his artist-fantasies yearn for the heights. But since moodiness and poverty prevent schooling, he contents himself with pursuing idle dreams about his future greatness; they expand his highly naïve self-consciousness. Even the work he envisions represents a dream which stimulates his fantasy through its mysteriousness tinged with the gruesome. He toys with the lethal and the secret, with a pleasure that increases as the rosiest thoughts and hopes assume reality in his imagination; his carefree view is oblivious to the dark shadows that already descend over his future. Only the others know that a consumptive illness will soon kill him.

A hectic blissful hope dangles over his dreams of the future, while death stands in the wings, giving Lyngstrand a melancholy cast. It sharply differentiates his self-conscious naïveté from the comedy of Ballested with his ridiculous self-contentment and myriad worthless skills. To be sure, Lyngstrand draws a smile from us, but we distinctly feel how near his figure is to the deep seriousness of the basic Ellida-problem. In fundamentally different ways, the same idea is replayed in the lives of both men: ambition without real creative strength and possibility for personal development is a vain choice; ambition which only dreams and toys loses its earnestness. Only Ellida's ambition is earnest because her idle dreaming and drifting fantasies are the first tentative steps toward growth. Startled and horrified, she comes out of her dreams to grasp desperately for truth and reality; and in her terrible inner struggles, the seductive illusions threaten to break into madness.

Mainly the emptiness of Lyngstrand and his lack of stature prevent him from becoming tragic. But the contrast between his joy of living and nearness to death has an almost symbolic effect; all his weak longings for freedom and satisfaction with misleading illusions are ironic, because behind them stands nothing. Nothingness, death, the gruesome alone become playthings which hide an actionless existence; they banish boredom for a few hours.

If such tendencies are found in a child—in little Hilde Wangel, Ellida's younger stepdaughter—understandably they can be quite pronounced. Secretly, Hilde clings to Ellida with idolizing love, but because she doubts Ellida's love, she stubbornly hides her feelings behind childish pranks and a pretended coldness. She is entirely at the mercy of growing up, and is unripe and incomplete; but perhaps also the incompleteness, the searching, and the becoming in Ellida attract Hilde. She senses that over Ellida hangs something fateful and puzzling, which awaits a solution. The excitement of that surmise gives her no peace and is further heightened when she learns that Ellida's mother had been "crazy." In the same way, she also comes close to Lyngstrand, because the contradiction between his confiding hopes and the certainty of his early death put her in a state of tension and unrest; she cannot resist talking to him often about that contradiction and thinking about it from different perspectives. Her curiosity stems as little from pity as from horror, but kernels of both lie in it. Since no one guides or educates her, she toys, in a troubled way, with her own inclinations. She has the need to stimulate herself with the mysterious, and therefore charming, aspect of life; her life is like the ancient crucian-pond that, so to speak, also encloses her own, small existence, and whose waters she whips up artificially to give them a semblance in her mind to a real sea. She is irresistibly attracted to elements in the character of her stepmother and in the fate of the young Lyngstrand. She has traits in common with Ellida. Of course, Hilde does not have the craving of a mature person for infinite growth; hers is only a curiosity peculiar to her youthful age—no mighty ebb and flow, only a crinkled wavelet in inland water. The horror which entices Ellida is toned down in Hilde and rendered harmless in her favorite expression, "Oh, I think that's so exciting." But the connection between horror and excitement remains nevertheless, pushing Hilde beyond surface attraction and mere objective curiosity toward a real injecting of herself into the exciting unknown. For that reason, she is not content with suspensefully watching her stepmother; this suspensefulness involuntarily turns into intense love which stubbornly demands reciprocity—Hilde wants to belong to Ellida.

Not with the same hidden sympathy does the older stepdaughter, Bolette, join Ellida, partly because she is already an adult, though with a relatively limited upbringing. As such, with more contained poise, she is able to face Ellida who is so severely, inwardly conflicted. Aside from that, Bolette is no longer able to view Ellida's situation with Hilde's childlike fascination with the "exciting" and the curious; with worry, she ponders the sorry consequences which Ellida's situation may have for her father's happiness and for their home—and, above all, also for her own future. It was her fervent wish to go out into the world, to explore it, to develop freely, and to let the world impress her. Obstructive to her desires is the fact that her father and her home do not receive the slightest support from Ellida. As a mature person, her expectations from life were far firmer than those of Hilde; they are

no dark, half-understood yearnings but are sensible and egotisti-
cally directed toward a definite goal. Instead of swinging and
playing on the cradling waves, with which Hilde still takes childish pleasure and contentment, Bolette's sure eye espies a boat
that can carry her into the distance. She justifies herself with
these words, "I find that I do have responsibilities toward myself."

But as much as her awareness of a goal separates her from the
others, she shares with the persons mentioned so far a
characteristic lack of strength. Still, Bolette's weak will, unlike
that of the others, is not based on the inability to give wishes for
life a defined form, but comes from a lack of courage. She does not
dare to follow these verses:

> On her own wings shall she dare the journey;
> then one will see if they will break or carry.*

While the others are led astray by the planless and adventurous,
she is incapable of withdrawing from the comfortable conventions of daily life in order to plunge into the unknown and the
possibly dangerous. This cautious and fearful rationality also
describes her conduct at home: she is efficient and busy but far
removed from the rebellious honesty of the little Hilde, and is
concerned up to the last with hiding her resentment against
Ellida, while giving her friendly co-operation.

Bolette is caught in the same passivity as the others, constantly awaiting outside help: "some kind of miracle" or "some
kind of happy turn of fate." "Oh, I have no real currents in me.
Probably, I have been meant to stay here in the crucian pond, I
think." Therefore, when the only boat that appears at her crucian
pond already has a boatsman who challenges her to take a cruise
jointly into the wide world, she allows herself to be persuaded
quite easily. So as not to face the world by herself and arduously
win her freedom, she even accommodates herself to a completely
new bond: marriage.

Bolette's former tutor and Ellida's former suitor, Arnholm,
proposes to her. Long and faithfully has he loved the lady from
the sea, and on his own, he would never have let his affections
turn to someone else. But a misunderstanding had led him to

---

*From Love's Comedy.

believe that Bolette loves him, and this mistake flatters his vanity so much that he feels himself bound to Bolette, even after she has enlightened him about matters. "Slowly I allowed myself the illusion," he said; ". . . there grew in me a lively and grateful affection for you. Your image . . . will always have the color and impress of the mood into which my illusion placed me."

And so, even Arnholm creates an arbitrary mirage of a future life; no more does he feel the need for using the truth as a basis for his new relationships than Bolette needs to ground her freedom in truth. But his deliberate self-deception has more success than his genuine affection for Ellida because it brings Bolette into his arms. If to the first loved-one he could not be "the stranger" who entices her onto the high seas of life, he succeeds well indeed with Bolette because he frees her from the narrow confines of her home. At any rate, "the stranger," even in small measure, meets Bolette's relatively modest imaginings: a well-to-do man with the gold-rimmed glasses of a slightly balding schoolmaster, a man who will enable her to make the loveliest trips throughout the wide world in order to satisfy her thirst for knowledge and allow her to learn geography first-hand.

As a matter of fact, it is not Arnholm but Lyngstrand who represents to her "the stranger." For Bolette, a little earlier, had promised Lyngstrand, during a superficial welling-up of sympathy, that she would think fondly of him until his return. That does not mean much because Lyngstrand—although he preens himself with her promise—flirts just as busily with Hilde before his departure. Ostensibly he will not seek to revenge bitterly the broken vow as will Ellida's real "stranger," in line with his convictions.

So we see that among the minor characters—Arnholm, Lyngstrand, Hilde, and Bolette—are played out all possible variations of the Ellida-theme in a comic vein that borders on farce. In a most surprising way, Bolette's figure is illuminated by irony. In a certain sense, Bolette belongs to those female figures whose striving for emancipation have up until now been portrayed with solemn seriousness: like Nora and Mrs. Alving, she strives for experience and life-awareness through release from a restrictive home. But this wish for freedom is ultimately expressed in her submission to bonds because it is so lovely "not to have to worry about the future and not to be concerned with dumb penny-pinching." She does not see her self-contradictions, because the freedom for which she strives is nothing more than an expeditious way of gaining a comfortable existence; her aim was pitched low enough. Here, Nora's and Mrs. Alving's ideal and mental cravings are converted into a philistine thirst for knowledge by a "more high-minded daughter" who longs for a teacher's diploma.

Because they are common and minor character types, their lack of self-education and self-restraint—which, in contrast, poses grave dangers to Ellida—can be treated with light irony. The great waves thunder and storm, while the wavelets quietly gurgle away in the sand.

But such play and giggling are at the same time the after-sounds of a tremendous and slowly fading seriousness, and are therefore able to prepare us for a new tragedy—like an overture that precedes the appearance of Ibsen's last great female figure: Hedda Gabler.

Those sounds, which were perceptible as side accompaniments, then swell visibly in the following Hedda-drama into a dominant ground-bass; but in the enormous contrast between neutralizing flirtation and that which it masks lies the transition from the jocular and harmless to the fateful and tragic.

The pervasive contradictions between wanting and accomplishing, between what people dream and achieve, are ironies that lie over all the minor characters in the Ellida-drama, and become pointed to the extreme in the main figure of Hedda Gabler. Hedda represents the highest tension of self-contradiction, embodied only by naïve and varied harmlessness in the others mentioned. She is an image of boundless demands for freedom and the decisive rejection of every duty and responsibility, an image allied with a weakness that yields to everything perishable and allows itself to be captured by the most trifling. Hedda finds herself halfway between wild and tame, vacillating between being free or bound, without the courage to accept the consequences of the polarity, or the reconciliation of it. This halfway position becomes an ironic paradox for Hedda: the inner promptings of a nature nominally born wild but pretending to be tame; it is her complete lack of motive power and self-definition that compels her contradictions.

In Hedda Gabler recurs the basic trait which characterized the immature Ellida: the absence of form and content, the negativity of her original dream of freedom. But what in Ellida was the result of an all-too-rich, almost sickly inwardness, which could only ripen slowly through a mature will, is in Hedda a lack of inwardness and the capacity to develop—hers is a poverty-stricken soul. The depth out of which Hedda must ascend is not filled with a life brimming like fathomless waves, but it is an empty depth, a void, where no great power slumbers. She does not appear to us like a creature who wrestles with her existence and vainly seeks to bring her inmost self into outer expression; on the contrary, she controls herself completely and is an all-hardened surface, a deceptive shell, a mask prepared for every occasion. Earlier Ibsen personages who bask in mock contentment have an air of superficiality touched by the comic, whereas Hedda's superficiality has strange tones: they resemble waltz tunes over the abyss of nothingness.

Instead of the sickly in Ellida's nature (which is healed only through a lengthy process), we find an entirely different mental condition, one that has the appearance of health and "clear, cold tranquility." Instead of a life-consuming fever, she possesses a lifeless iciness or life-weakness bordering on death, whose existence-demands become weaker as the demands rise more greedy and boundless. She resembles a clawing wolf within a sheep's skin who has traded predatory physical strength for an exclusively predatory spirit. Condemned to a life of tameness and the ordinary, she fearfully avoids every act of daring; with impotent anger and inner savageness, she toys with her own longing for freedom, as a timorous hand plays with weapons. She has no target and would not know how to hit it, even if she had one; so she had to content herself with a toy that would, at least, help her overcome the tedium of inactivity: "I stand here idly and shoot into the blue sky!" becomes her motto. A "letting herself go" is the only positive trend that remains in her life's ideals—the freedom to engage in the destructive caprice of the moment.

That ordinary mental attitude of the average person stands opposed to the more sober content of superior minds. For the superior person is still capable of developing a free life and reconciling that world with the world of the attic, or being capable of participating also in the battle between them. Excluded from both worlds is the cowardly creature who farcically absorbs these contentious elements, but only makes of them a comical counterpart to the truthful overcoming and wedding of those elements, as is evident in Ellida's triumphant words: "Free and responsible." For a person like Hedda, there remains nothing except to creep away cautiously into the protectiveness of a well-ordered attic life where she will be sheltered from dangerous storms, and where she will not have to endure trials of strength; in the silence of the attic, however, unnoticed and therefore unreprimanded, she can nibble on forbidden fruits. Such a person waits with bored passivity until coincidence brings a stimulant which allows a breath of fresh air but does not allow the light of truth to penetrate into one's life. For that person shuns the light, although yearning for freedom; that person attempts to join poles in a terrifying compromise.

"Shade and fresh air, both." . . . "Oh, a whole ocean of light is streaming in. (She draws the curtains together.) That will give me a softer light," we hear a female voice say. With these words, Hedda stands—as if unmasked—in the morning sun, while the autumn leaves fall from the trees outside.

The light of morning and autumn rest upon her. For, with her near-childish, spiritual and moral immaturity, she wishes us to believe in the illusory beginning of growth of a creature who still has to unlearn her destructive and petty whims that reduce everything near her to the value of toys. Here is not the unreadiness of a Nora in her doll house. Hedda is not unripe, but rather is like an all-too-early decayed autumn, as she returns to the narrow perspectives of a child and its playful self-seeking. . . .

Well does she possess inclinations for destruction, but they have nothing in common with the daemonic and elementary force of Rebecca's nature (in *Rosmersholm*) that in the storm of a great passion indiscriminately and relentlessly drives forth good as well as evil, both the ignoble and the noble. What could have surfaced from the nature of a Hedda, except bored and therefore irritable mischief that stems from petty motives? What we learn about her early life is in fact of an impotent jealousy directed toward someone else's attractiveness: it is her jealous annoyance that prompted her habitually to pull the hair of a schoolmate,

Thea Rysing, because she had a more comely head of curly hair. Something of that annoyance pursues her throughout life; as soon as she thinks about that firm, luminous curly hair, she is gripped by a wild urge, which she had mastered only with great effort earlier, to burn off Thea's hair. But only seldom does her mischievousness translate itself into action, only when it can occur in a non-dangerous way; only when she has nothing to fear from a defenseless opponent, does she allow herself unrestraint: "something comes over me, before I realize it. And then, I cannot let go of it."

These words—spoken during Hedda's first entrance—are related to her devious attribution of illness to the old maiden aunt, Miss Tesman, because of her outmoded dress. But significantly enough, even here she hides her malicious intentions behind a measured politeness and a smooth mask which she never discards.

In the home of her father, the old General Gabler, she had the opportunity of practicing control over outward appearance. Such "good form" and outward behavior are somewhat similar to the upbringing of others in moralistic patriarchal traditions and binding duties. Here, as there, the content of upbringing may seem similar, but in the first case the emphasis is exclusively on outer form; and with that, the dispositions behind this formally correct life are given wider latitude than otherwise possible. True, Hedda grows up in an attic-world full of fearful biases and narrowly drawn boundaries, but her concern was less to be at home there than to appear to be so. Her attic resembles, so to speak, a salon which one entered more or less masked, and to which one suited one's behavior: illusion and substance fall apart. Next to the compulsion to behave in a prescribed way in the eyes of the world, Hedda retains the freedom to do as she wishes; unencumbered by burdensome responsibilities, she plays away her girlhood with dressing-table toiletries, balls, excursions and visits to spas. This kind of existence is perfectly suited to her and she never protests against it. Hedda is Ibsen's only female figure whose experiences do not contain struggle or growth toward the new; on the contrary, she perseveres in that early-given life form because self-contradictions have room within it. She clings, like Bolette, to the accustomed and the inherited; but without Bolette's efficient activities, Hedda is only concerned with superficialities. Like Hilde and Lyngstrand, she possesses an inclination toward the wildly adventurous, but since she lacks a zest for life, she withdraws into a shell and hides carefully all impulses that could damage her reputation. She lets her gaze wander into the open world, with a peeking and lusting curiosity, but will only allow her thoughts, enlightened as she is, to play with forbidden fruit.

For that reason, Hedda as a young girl carefully protects herself against anything which might compromise her. Even though she would dearly have given herself over to sensual pleasures, she satisfies herself with a comradely relationship with the young Eilert Lövborg who—profligate and deviate as he was—knew how to tell her about a world of seduction, the unclean and the forbidden. At a time when Nora and Mrs. Alving, during their youth, exhaust themselves in the pursuit of truth, we see Hedda and her friend sit on the corner sofa every afternoon, "for want of a picture album and with ever the same illustrated newspapers" before them, completely absorbed in Lövborg's secret confessions, while unsuspectingly "over by the window" the old General sat reading his papers.

Eilert Lövborg belongs to those male types, among them also Ulric Brendel, whose first representative perhaps was Falk in *Love's Comedy*. Despite their call to greatness and their boldly striking out of the narrows onto the high seas of life, they lack a firm hand on the helm. And so they are unsteady, "driven by storm and wind. And after a while, they sink deeper and deeper." But they do possess the courage of being themselves. . . .

Understandably, matters go so far that the cautious camaraderie of Lövborg's relationship with Hedda no longer suffices. At the point "when the threatening danger of reality could enter the relationship," it becomes evident how far Hedda is removed from being serious about her desire for freedom. As soon as Lövborg confidently broaches intimacy, she shrinks back and threatens to shoot him down with her father's pistols. But she shrinks back even from that. And after Lövborg parts from her, she also confesses that only cowardice had prevented her from giving herself to him: "I have such a horrid fear of scandal!"

Thus Hedda's inclination, as far as one can call it that in view of her nature, is directed towards Lövborg, except that attraction and repulsion are for her inextricably entwined; a horror mixes itself with the enticement that exudes from him. Naturally, it is not the same horror that overcomes Ellida when she is confronted by the stranger, nor is it a premonitory resistance of a mind capable of growing beyond the empty allure of adventurousness. Such an undoubtedly ethical moment, under the impact of horror, would elude Hedda completely because she does not experience such far-reaching growth. She does not even suspect that possibility, for every ideal which combines self-restraint and responsibility is repugnant to her: "Don't talk to me about things like responsibilities." Her fear of responsibilities and of joining with Lövborg as "the stranger" forms a parody of the mysterious Ellida-shudder. As Hedda often reminds one of a distorted image of Ellida, her "shuddering" is the fear of appearing compromised in her social circle.

What she admires above all, albeit secretly, is the courage of immoderation and the pleasure from the submission of self of which Lövborg is capable; she feels clearly that these would express her ideals of life, if only she were not "so terribly cowardly" to permit herself to follow those impulses to the end. "Yes, courage . . . yes! If only one would have it!"—she laments. If only she would have the courage to despise and strip herself of everything in which her being is confined, as in a restricting corset: one's correct bearing and impeccable deportment and the aesthetic impress of formats sanctioned by society. She cannot extricate herself from that narrow prison; through her weakness she is condemned to remain a tame Hedda with wild urges. In her view, however, a "shimmer of natural beauty" drops over that which is "the courageous act," one which falls outside the frame of the correct and the boring. For that reason, Lövborg, even with all his shabbiness and dissoluteness, seems to her in no way ugly, but quite naturally an ideal person, "warm and happy, with vine-leaves in his hair."

Because Hedda is inexperienced in such matters, she also is not able to save Lövborg from "drowning." It is a woman with a completely different mind who extends a helping hand: Hedda's erstwhile schoolmate, Thea Rysing, whom she envied for her shocks of curly hair. Thea is the second wife of the old district-judge, Elvsted, whose domestic household she managed and whose children she had brought up. He had married her, as she says, "because my keep was not expensive . . . I am a bargain." They never grew to love each other because "he certainly never had affection for anyone but himself." She also admits that "we never had any ideas in common." Without talent or other outstanding attributes, Thea led a hard, joyless life silently devoted to carrying out duties. The greatest wish that occupies her mind nevertheless involves no demand for pleasure and freedom but only a longing for a real task and a real home: "Oh, if I could only have a home! But I have none, and never had one." What she finds most difficult is to preserve the illusory existence of her marriage. She wishes to assume with all truthfulness some task, some love; she wishes to become necessary and effective for some other human being.

Among all those persons grouped around Ellida or Hedda, Thea is one of the most modest, one of the least wild-natured or free-born. But her desire for the real, and her drive to transpose her entire inner life onto a plane of genuineness, lift her uniquely into high relief against all pleasure-seekers and illusion-filled characters.

When Lövborg comes to Elvsted's home as tutor for Thea's stepchildren, he gains the highest admiration for her selfless efficiency. In her need to be meaningful to others and to be of service, regardless of personal gain, she forms so great a contrast to his self-indulgence that this made a deep impression upon him. Looking at her, he was taken with shame and learned to adopt voluntary moderation and responsibility.

"He abandoned his old habits," Thea said. "Not because I asked him to, for I never dared to ask him that. But he noticed that his old habits were repugnant to me. And so, he let go of them."

Never did he talk with Thea about those things which Hedda found of exclusive interest, "because of all those things she was ignorant." But while he was making the effort to awaken and shape her awareness, his own youngest ideals again rose to the surface. That which had been soiled and disfigured within him by loose living, he now sees mirrored in its original purity in Thea's receptive spirit. And so he succeeds, in her company to be sure, to complete a philosophical-cultural study, which fills him with

pride and restored confidence: the book is the child of a true
spiritual marriage. On the basis of this book, he ventures to build
a new and better life, for "Thea's pure soul was in this book." And
when he returns with his book in order to regain his place in the
city where Hedda lives, Thea follows him. She tears the bonds
that fasten her, despite the disapproval of the world, because she
knows that Lövborg needs her. As timid and modest as she is, she
has courage at the center of her love; "tremendous courage when
it comes to being a comrade," Lövborg says of her. And Hedda
asks with amazement: "But, dear Thea, how could you have
dared! What do you think people will say about you?" But Mrs.
Elvsted replies confidently: "In God's name, let them say what
they want! Because I have done nothing other than what I had to
do."

It is interesting that in this drama, with its sharp condemnation of emasculated strivings for freedom, we are suddenly reminded of Nora and the justification of a genuine and irrepres-
sible drive for freedom that courageously faces the world. Even
more interesting and significant than the purely external and
comparable situation of Thea is a certain similarity to the Ellida-
conflict and its entirely opposite solution. Neither consideration
for her husband nor for her stepchildren holds Thea back. The
lofty dream of the future, which hovers before her, is no vague
longing for freedom, like Ellida's, but an understood and precious duty, a responsibility accepted with a full heart, toward
another human being who is in need of her help. Her ability to
break loose and to rebel against convention has developed from
the same drive for responsibility that earlier prompted her to live
in an entrusted circle. By way of contrast, despite Hedda's
enlightenment and freedom-longing, she remains dependent
upon all that is inherited and conventional. So we see Thea, who
originally possessed the spirit of the attic, assertively representing freedom and truth, while Hedda now represents a willfulness
that hides terrified behind the walls of an attic world.

It is significant that the man who married Hedda had earlier
been interested in Thea; both belong to the inhabitants of the
attic, and eventually though, they will possess more substance
than Hedda ever did. Hedda calls her husband a "specialist," that
is, one whose understanding extends only to that which can

neatly fit into ready-made pigeon holes. Like Hjalmar Ekdal in *The Wild Duck,* he is brought up by two maiden-aunts who pampered and admired him tenderly, but unlike Ekdal, he did not fall prey to vanity but became a "good-hearted soul." The modest bearing and selfless kindness of these women also influenced his personality; their need constantly "to have someone to live for" also awakened in him a sense of true devotion for work and an undemanding sense of duty, tendencies which are diametrically opposite to those of Hjalmar's illusion-filled existence. Without independent ideas, and being receptive and imitative, he is always laden with technical journals and voluminous collections from various archives; he busily anticipates uncut volumes: "It is pure pleasure to cut those leaves!" Even with his first appearance, we already intuit that it is his happiest mission to encourage the significant work of another person through selfless labor or to reconstruct it, as will become evident at the end of the play when we believe in his hearty promise "to dedicate his life to it."

Hedda's actual superiority comes not from being more talented than Tesman—but it rests on his unpretentiousness and simplicity; he is much less spoiled than she. He has wedded her because he really loved and admired her, and she followed him after she had literally "danced herself into tiredness," and because he had seriously meant to do well by her: "That was truly more than what my other admirers were prepared to do," she admits. The others shied away from marrying a capricious, spoiled girl who only had dancing and horse riding on her mind. While the old district-judge married his Thea because she was inexpensive, Tesman married Hedda, despite the fact that she was an expensive and costly luxury—and his entire happiness consists of giving her whatever is in his power. Completely against his nature, he gambles on the uncertain possibility of a job and plunges into debt; what mattered most to him was to see her happy and in good spirits. It is like a pictorial representation of his simple and trusting love of her that, in the second act, he serves her with these words: "It is such great fun to wait on you, Hedda."

For her part, she has completely deceived him from the start. To condition him for marriage, she used her instinct to wax enthusiastic about her longing for a home they would share in common. Through various sacrifices, he manages to procure that home for her. But privately she had something else in mind: an open house, socializing, high-society courting, servants in livery, and a saddle horse. Only such things could in any case banish in her eyes the boredom of "always and forever being together with one and the same person." She wishes no deeper understanding of the "one and the same" person who is her husband, and nothing seems to her to be so superfluous as Thea's wish for companiable work and a joint mission in life. While a book becomes the spiritual child conceived by Lövborg and Thea, reflecting their seriousness and the inner necessity of their life-bond, Hedda experiences, with some justification, her impending maternity as the essence of the ludicrous and accidental, and as a personalized parody of her being and desires. Just as a child is a sign of the marriage of two opposites joined by an inner unity, so then infertility is a sign of self-contradiction that harbors the irreconcilable. For Hedda therefore, the horrible and the plainly unbearable lie in the challenge to create—to create a life through which a circle of ideal duty is rounded out of its own being. Out of this existence, eternally emptied of productiveness, no road leads back into the fullness of reality and the fruitful life; and since an absolute life-emptiness contains a contradiction, Hedda quite consistently says about herself: "Sometimes it seems as if I have a talent for only one thing in this world . . . to bore myself to death."

But of necessity, this enormous emptiness directly turns into the most materialistic pleasure-seeking of which fantasy is capable, crawling on the soil of the everyday and searching for every momentary stimulus. The "gourmandizing" of the sybaritic world, which has some intellectual sense and finds affinity with Ulric Brendel and Eilert Lövborg, has lost every last vestige of intellectuality in Hedda's mind; her exclusive concern is with material well-being. Quite characteristic of that is the brief scene in which she learns that Tesman's pecuniary situation would neither permit a livery-outfitted servant nor a saddle horse. Immediately she threatens with her pistols: "Well, at any rate, I do have something to entertain myself with meanwhile." That not only has a childish effect but also a symbolic one; we feel, at this point, how eerily close a Hedda stands to death and how eerily meager is the life sustenance on which she feeds—it would take only the wind of coincidence to scatter the few inconsequentials of her life and to extinguish its sense.

As we see Hedda toying or yawning, we also note that this reflects a serious attitude of mind, which forms the starting point of her tragic end. She feels revulsion and fright at the burgeoning life within her maternal body and she stares into a dark emptiness that responds with pure negation. Of these silent thoughts that find her constantly close to the border of desperation, hardly one becomes perceptible, except that now and then her clenching of fists and an angry glance break the studied calmness of her behavior. That mood of dark seriousness surrounds her just as the autumn surrounds the house and showers its yellow leaves upon the windows. Her forced gaiety appears similarly artificial and faded, evident further in the innumerable bouquets lying on the tables: "All rooms here seem to smell of lavender and dried roses. . . . There is an odor of mortality about it. It reminds me of bouquets—the day after the ball."

In her search for constantly new ways of cheering herself up and finding distractions, she finally rediscovers a friend who promises to be as entertaining as Lövborg once was, "being able to entertain with all sorts of different subjects." He is a friend of the house: Counselor Brack. The difference between him and Lövborg consists, in this case, only in that she will be even less satisfied, especially since the pistols now are only used for merry practice shooting. Hedda poses only one condition: he must preserve all decorum and not demand of her that she compromise herself. But he too poses a condition: he is to take his place in a triangle and that he would not have to share her with others. In return, he would save her from the yawning boredom of a twosome journey through life in which she does not dare at times to step down from the railway carriage in order to move about a little, for "there is always someone standing by" to look at one's legs. And so, unnoticed, there steps into the carriage "the third person, in order to join the pair inside. . . . And then, the train moves on." Something of the freedom for which she secretly wishes as a young girl, she gains for herself precisely by letting herself in for the burdensome captivity of marriage, for she does not possess the courage to be truthfully free—open and without restraint; she becomes free only through a deception which protects her. Ideals of truth and freedom have perversely turned into their opposites: into an undesired non-freedom in the service of untruth.

The alliance that the Counselor enters into with Hedda is in danger of dissolving almost as soon as it was formed. Hedda meets Lövborg again and her interest in the companion of her youth is rekindled through a strong motive power—envy. Hedda cannot get over the fact that Thea succeeded in strongly influencing Lövborg, and she exerts herself to win power over him again. Through Thea's help, Lövborg was restored to a sober, orderly life, but now Hedda succeeds in regaining power as she induces his earlier drinking habits. She tries to awaken in him the feeling that it is ridiculous and unworthy of a male to fear temptation and timidly avoid her. The caution which Thea advised seems to Hedda solely a petty failure of nerve because she can visualize freedom and maleness only in terms of letting oneself go—her picture of the ideal. But it is noteworthy that while she appeals to Lövborg's "male dignity," she actually and instinctively taunts him for cowardice in fearing to be more conventional. There lies in her actions a characteristic contradiction from which she can never free herself because it is an intrinsic part of herself.

Lövborg meanders between the influence of the two women. Prompted by Hedda, Lövborg celebrates by attending a banquet given by Counselor Brack. On the way from Brack to the house of a citywide known beauty, he loses the irreplaceable manuscript of a work upon which hinge all his hopes. Tesman finds the manuscript in the street, brings it home, and gives it for brief keeping to his wife. But Hedda cannot repress the urge to do with the work what she had dearly wanted to do earlier with Thea's curly hair: to burn it. Although she has nothing to gain from this and regards it not even as a hoped-for means to some goal or other, she still has the satisfaction of destroying what she could not have created, so that through this act others will experience the same bleakness and hopelessness which confronts her day and night. She cannot tolerate the sight of this "child of a true spiritual marriage," she who feels with horror and reluctance the stirring of life within her.

"Now I am burning your child, Thea! . . . You with the curly hair! Your and Eilert Lövborg's child. Now I burn . . . now I burn the child."

To Tesman, she excuses her crime through her all-too-great love for him and her fear of seeing him overshadowed by Lövborg's intellectual feat; she suppresses a smile at his happy gullibility. In fact, he was overjoyed at her explanation of what had happened, although he was shocked and chagrined by an act he would gladly have prevented; that she really loved him is for Tesman a happy admission which makes it impossible to remain angry with her for long. Hedda awakens here the deceitful illusion of an act, committed in fact by Nora, through which her professed love becomes a culpable act. And Tesman, for his part, acts in a manner which Nora had wished from her husband, Helmer. Tesman hears only the note of love in Hedda's admission, and we do not doubt for a moment that if the necessity arises he will take his wife's guilt upon himself and protect her with his name and honor. Later, he does take her expiation upon himself. This Nora-sentiment, which is carried over in some respects onto the conventional person of Tesman, reminds us of how much nearer the conventional can come to the truly ideal than the distorted and perverted Hedda-figure, who is an exception to the common-run of humanity. So it does not seem surprising to us to find again features that seemed to have been borrowed from that weak person Helmer, and to find similar mouthings: "I don't wish to see anything having to do with sickness and death. Let me be spared from everything that is repulsive."

The instinctive drawing back from every conflict with the judgments of society estranges Hedda very rapidly again from Lövborg, the comrade of her youth. After he has compromised himself and foolishly lost a newly-won public respect, Hedda allows herself to be persuaded easily by the jealous Brack that hence she must avoid Lövborg. "Every decent home will be closed again to Eilert Lövborg from now on," consequently, and above all, her home as well. She is no Thea who will want to share his shame, consoling and helping him. When Lövborg refuses Thea's help, she cries out: "What then is my life good for!" Hedda instead looks for a way of getting rid of him. When in desperation he expresses his intent of putting an end to his dissolute life, he may be meeting her secret wishes. Although she burns his manuscript only after this scene, she allows him to believe that the work is lost. She does not speak one word which would revive all his hopes; if Thea had inspired him to a new life, Hedda's help would not be missing in the act of death. To the cowardly Hedda, suicide looms as a picture of completed heroism, as a picture of "beauty." With that, she gives Lövborg one of her pistols, as a token of remembrance, and begs him to make sure that his suicide occurs with "beauty."

Lövborg gratefully receives the weapon from her hand, but his end is other than Hedda had wished. He does not shoot himself, nor was this visit to Hedda his last of the evening. He is later found dead in the boudoir of a notorious singer he had sought out that night, suspecting perhaps that his manuscript was on her premises. The pistol, accidentally discharged or triggered by another's hand, was found in his breast-pocket. He lay there with his belly torn open, rather than with a shot through his breast or temple as envisioned in Hedda's heroic picture. He is even suspected of being a thief because the weapon does not belong to him. "Oh, how laughable and mean. A curse lies over everything I touch!" cries Hedda when she learns the facts.

But even her own fate is touched by this death. Brack knows of the role played by Hedda; and now she is delivered into his hand, the hand of a conscienceless man. Only he can prevent her from being held as much responsible as the lady of notoriety. "Do you believe that all this will be exposed?" she asks Brack. And she receives this answer: "No, Hedda Gabler . . . not as long as I keep silent."

By his daring to use her maiden name, one can already sense the price he will exact for his silence. For he knows that even more unbearable for her is the threatening scandal, "the scandal of which you are in such mortal terror." And he is not mistaken in that; from such scandal she wishes to escape at all cost. But she is just as firmly determined not to be dependent upon him: "Unfree. Unfree then! . . . No . . . That thought I cannot endure! Never."

Those are Hedda's loveliest words throughout the drama. Even though her entire freedom signifies something worthless, and though she limits herself to an arbitrary and boring submission to whim—which has neither the strength to seek true abandonment in pleasure nor to assume obligations voluntarily—still, it follows from what she says that freedom is for her a summit, higher even than life. Even if she had not understood how to take advantage of the freedom in her life, except in pursuit of her own momentary whims, still she would never submit to the whims of others. In other respects, she does know how to meet threatening dependencies by raising herself fearlessly to a true plane of independence, despite knowing that she is ever enslaved by her weaknesses. Only one thing remains open to her: to withdraw from life itself.

The glance Hedda casts—once more—upon her home and her husband, in her leavetaking, works with a shattering effect; it is a glance that reveals to her eyes, with glaring clarity, that life itself has in a certain fashion exiled her.

With Thea at his side, Tesman sits at the table. In the light of the lamp lie all of Lövborg's surviving notes and scrap papers, which they located in order to reconstruct his destroyed work as accurately as Thea's memory and joint effort will permit. To that work, Tesman will dedicate himself and will perform it with the conscientiousness natural to him. Although he is better suited to build on the work of others than to create independently, the honest sympathy of his heart spurs him on, in this case, to his utmost abilities: "It will work out! It must work! . . . My own research will have to wait in the meantime . . . That is something that I owe to the memory of Eilert." Since the debt is incurred for Hedda's sake, he says, "Hedda, you do understand me?" But what he does for her, by expiating her wrongdoing, leaves her completely indifferent. Only Thea and not Hedda can help with the demanding chores; he will work busily with Thea and spend his evenings with her, while she—with her love for the deceased—will continuously inspire him.

"Oh, God, if I could only inspire your husband in the same way," she remarks to her friend, and Tesman readily responds, "I really think that I am beginning to feel something of this kind."

"Is there nothing," asks Hedda, "that I can do to be of use to you two?"

"No, absolutely nothing," Tesman assures her. The only one who is free to converse and entertain her is Counselor Brack. Unconsciously, a verdict had been pronounced upon her: to do his best work, and as a consequence of his great love for her, Tesman must turn from her and be with the other woman. Here then converge all activity and efficiency, all real content and bearing, of two conventional people. It does not matter whether or not Hedda comes or goes, she is completely superfluous, used up: life will close up behind her without a gap.

Then, Hedda slowly walks into the dark back room, where her piano stands and on which rests her pistol case. Through the opening of the drapes, a friendly, peaceful picture around her lamp-lit work table presents itself, and she feels herself to be an outcast standing alone in the dark. The picture she views contains only a small, undemanding idyll, an attic-idyll perhaps, but yet it is a picture of hopeful and life-filled reality, from which strength and love will emanate. Only she must stand and blush at the sight, because for her no such reality exists any longer, which could have served as a beginning point for her.

Working at the table, they suddenly hear a dance played on the piano coming from the back room, something wildly out of tune, which breaks into their concentrated and blissful earnestness. No one has any idea that in these frivolously gay chords everything is gathered that expresses Hedda's empty existence— a passing glitter that leaves no traces. With eerie mockery these tones are reminders of pictures from the dim past: Nora arises before us as she, with a deadly decision in her heart, is compelled to dance the *tarantella*. But for her, the deathlike darkness is filled with the supernatural glow of the "wondrous" and with sacred sounds that drown out the wild music. That "wondrous" element in Nora's dreams of life appears in Hedda's life. It strains to be parodied as much as "the terrifying" in the longings and dreams of Ellida on the road of personal independence toward ideals embodied by Ibsen's early heroines, just as the renunciation of the self is embodied in the last ones. For it is an act of self-renunciation, in a dark and ironic sense, through which Hedda rings down her life: she does not die for another person as does Rebecca, and she does not live for another person as does Ellida— she dies for herself as she had lived for herself. In that she dies, she proves herself to be among those free born, untamed creatures; for in the necessity of her death, there first is revealed the whole tragedy of the uncanny contradiction of Hedda Gabler:

the tragic aspect is that Hedda may only prove to herself the true existence of her inner freedom by cancelling herself out. She extinguishes the life of the tame and false Hedda, caught in the meshes of her own weakness, who while still living would not have found bearable the verdict now intoned by Counselor Brack over the deceased: "People don't do such things!"

In the dark, Hedda lies on the sofa, with a pistol pressed to her temple. Throughout her life she has toyed with that weapon—the shot into the blue sky was the symbol of a drive for freedom, but it was without inner truth, strength, or target, and therefore without value. The pistol shot reaches the sole target of possible worth; it wins the only truth possible through the power ever to set itself up as a target:

a shot—and nothingness.

Epilogue: A FABLE

O NCE there was an attic.
Low and slanted walls reached down toward wooden floor boards, and the daylight had to find its way laboriously through cobwebbed dormer windows and cracks. But over those boards, hay was spread carefully and a water-filled barrel was placed there. For here, people held all kinds of animals captive and weaned them from the life of nature through domestication and care. Fowls of every sort cackled, goitered doves cooed on the metal rim of the barrel, and tumbler pigeons fluttered from their nests under the roof constructions. Far down, however, in the straw, frightened squirrels crawled under the brittle conifer nee- dles of several Christmas trees that were to represent a forest, although the leftover colorful tinsel of the previous Christmas still clung to their branches.

In a half-darkened corner stood a newly-woven basket which was upholstered comfortably and with special care. For it shel- tered the noblest of all creatures deprived of their freedom, name- ly, a wild duck and therefore "a truly wild" bird. It seemed not only to be the noblest but also the most pitiable amongst them all. Though its fellow creatures willingly adapted themselves to an artificial idyll, isn't it surely and necessarily a tragedy for a bird of the wild to be confined to an attic?

For that question, we have six answers and six stories.

* * *

Nora

PERHAPS, as a small helpless bird, she was taken from a maternal nest and put among domestic animals. Brought up without any knowledge of her true nature and original home, and surrounded with constant pampering and preferential treatment, she enjoys herself innocently in her attic, which is like a large, gay playroom. What she discovers there through the eyes of a wild bird does not

give the impression of a real world, but shows an artificial imita-
tion of such a world, which serves as a welcome playground with
colorful toys for her childlike strength. So, she slowly becomes
adjusted. Yet there is woe when the season has approached
whose storms rattle the dormer windows and eventually tear
them open with a gust of abrupt force, suddenly revealing to the
small wild duck a view of heaven and earth. With the first flood of
light that unhaltingly sweeps over her, there comes also remembrance and recognition. With the first full stream of air that
breaks into the damp room of wooden boards, there also intrudes
what seems like a greeting waving from an intuited distance; it is
like the fragrant breath from an original home that lies far beyond
all the rooftops of the city with their chimney smoke, high and
away over all attics and prisons. She still does not know as yet
where her home is, only that it cannot be here; and so, her
undeniable instinct and a deep, mighty longing commandingly
force her wings into motion. And soon it is no longer a question if
the unpracticed wings can carry the wild duck and if there was a
path ahead through the beckoning distance; for there is no longer
a question of what remains behind—the ill-will and sorrow of the
others, their anger or tameness—for the duck silently spreads her
wings and floats into the measureless unknown, exchanging the
large playroom for the All.

* * *

Mrs. Alving

PERHAPS the little wild duck is not destined for such a fortunate
fate. No storm comes to tear open the gates of her prison, nor any
gust of wind blows them down with sudden force. So she grows
up, lives, ages, and finally passes away—ever in the same attic.
Through careful training, she had been taught that the worm-
pocked wooden walls were unscaleable barriers and that the
discipline and category of the domestic animal world was to be
regarded as nature's law. She was taught to regard the constructed surroundings, that resemble a stage set, as the big and
only reality, beside which no other any longer exists. Slowly she
accommodated and subordinated herself to the surroundings,
and strove hard to emulate the obedience and satisfied comfort of
the tame animals; she wanted to inhibit the strong and busy wing

that suddenly spread in the wondrous dreams of night and impatiently beat against the moldy walls. But all patient efforts fail. For the knowledge of her homeland, of the wilds and freedom, penetrates the attic. Even if freedom cannot come loudly and suddenly with the releasing force of a storm, still it sneaks in softly as an ever-returnihg, quiet messenger. The sun's rays bring that knowledge. They are awaited daily and eagerly, even by the domestic animals, if not as messengers from some distant and more beautiful land, then as a welcome transfiguration of their attic world. The rays cast an hallucinatory shimmer over the old rubbish; they tease luminous reflections from the clouded water of the barrel; and they cause the cobwebs and dust clouds to flash brightly and glimmer like clear strands of gold; their warm glow over the dried-up Christmas trees is like the reflections of spring.

But an entirely different message reaches the wild duck. The sun rays do not beautify the duck's surroundings; on the contrary, they reveal with sharp glare the whole stage-world of illusion, casting a merciless light that relentlessly and vividly glides over the naked poverty of the attic room, revealing every last sad aspect, down to the most hidden crevices hitherto protected by the veil woven by twilight. The wild duck follows the light rays with deep horror and longing, for it has brought recognition and disillusionment; she understands slowly that her own eyes—a wild bird's eyes that look about angrily and painfully—were meant to view the sun and the heights with integrity. She realizes that she lives in a world full of illusions, and that the true world lies far distant behind the blind windows through which the sun's light comes.

Dreamlike, in unclear quivering outlines, there rises before her a picture of that reality, like a rippling and whispering from distant waters and forests, like hovering flight under a wide, silent sky. And gradually that picture gains luster and color and fragrance and light, conjured up through the wild energy of desperation and yearning, until it stands there, almost graspable, so warm and strongly converted to breathing life that the surrounding theatrical world seems to evaporate into a disembodied ghostly being. In the midst of the cackling and chattering of her domestic companions, in the midst of the dust and the shabby confines of the wooden partitions, the wild duck dreams herself into being inwardly united with thousands of blissful, free-born swarms that wing their way unencumbered over the earth and toward the light of the sun.

Who would say that in this dream perception there does not truly lie release for the wild bird, a liberation that lifts her over restrictive barriers, while at the same time she dies, her thirsting eyes searchingly directed toward the sun, and with drooping wings crouching lonely among the sorrowing ghosts amid the withered Christmas trees?

* * *

Hjalmar and Hedwig—the Songbird

BUT PERHAPS it was a wild duck which did not in the least mind its life-long captivity. During the course of a hunt, it may have been hit under its wings by a load of buckshot; it may have sunk to the bottom of the water and held onto seaweeds with its beak, until a sharp-nosed retriever found it and brought it to the hunter. At first, it feels estranged among the domesticated animals in the attic, but then it meets a young songbird which permitted itself to be captured, for it was blind. Its blindness disguised the poverty and constrictedness of the attic world; and yet, its instinctive inclination toward the wild duck, which also originated in freedom under the sunshine, prompts it to cower on a twig and warble its sweetest songs for the duck.

Yet the other animals as well outdid themselves in showing the widely travelled stranger their admiration, and they felt honored when he decides to join them. He receives their best care and the choicest morsels; and that, surely, was far more pleasant than becoming outside, in the wilds, a tasty morsel for some birds of prey. With lame wings, withdrawn because of freedom's dangers, he therefore easily adjusts himself to a comfortable prison. The good food and restricted mobility encourage fat and laziness, and this gradually has a debilitating, soporific effect upon longing, unrest and ambition. In the damp air, lungs that had once breathed in rapid flight against the storm now became short-breathed; flight itself deteriorates into a chickenlike fluttering. Nothing any longer reminds them of the free, wild life of nature, except the sweet tones of the little songbird, amid the cackling of the domestic animals. To be sure, the old pictures of memory arise every time with the bird's tones, but they have changed long since from pain and sorrow to pleasantries that kill time and to smiling vanity that favors playing and boasting. So the captive wild bird preens himself by spreading his wounded wings against the dusty windows and showing the others how courageously he once challenged the storms by hovering under dark, moving clouds. But now he takes his ease in the fact that he is truly safe in the circle of good-natured doves and chickens and that no cloud moves above him, except in the shape of the downwind smoke of the free-standing chimney, that no lightning bolt flashes overhead, except as the flurry of sparks from the gray dust of the kitchen hearth.

Only one among them who delighted in the theatric representation of the wild duck regards the sham-promise of the drive for freedom as quite real. The small, blind songbird takes it seriously that her poor, captive comrade vainly tries to unfold his shattered wings once more in free flight. While in the grip of her wish to help him learn again how to move his wings and conquer freedom, he forgets himself and his own helpless blindness; he forgets his never-understood limitations: gropingly he spreads his feathers, rises, entangles himself in the dense darkness and the old, treacherous rubbish, and with broken wings plunges to the floor.

* * *

Rebecca

BUT PERHAPS it is also the wild duck herself who commits suicide in the narrow prison. Perhaps it proved futile that she had so completely ensconced herself and had flown voluntarily, moreover, into this prison. That wild duck is a lively and bold bird to whom it seems enticing to dominate among the weak and tamed creatures, and to try her luck. To be able to regain freedom at her discretion, she relies on the proven and practiced strength of her beak and limbs. Her intentions succeed beyond expectations. Her superior strength intimidated the domestic creatures and ruthlessly pushed aside every obstacle and opposition, so that soon everyone bows and submits. As for the confusion and destruction of an established order this necessarily brings about, the wild duck displays no particular concern. After all, her very presence brings with it a completely new law in place of hitherto established propriety—the rule of the stronger. Her weaker companions could not take revenge upon her.

But yet they did take revenge.

Not, of course, through means of counterforce and enmity; in those respects she remains superior. Much more than that, through their love and friendship they bind the wild bird ever more strongly to themselves. And precisely through that situation, the hidden danger becomes effective: it is the danger of the influence of the tame upon the wild, and the infection of the strong by those weakened through the danger of habituation. Though born in freedom, she is not one with the birds of prey in looking for victims among the domestic animals. For in the outside wilds, she had lived in contention with others; actually, she stands in closer relation to those creatures who are capable of adapting themselves to the world of humans. She is all-too-near them and has become constricted in that relationship. The bond that ties her to the tame animals is as effective as a gunshot which downs one accurately and helplessly, or it is like a rope around one's neck, which threatens slowly to strangle one's strength.

Much too long she lingers in the oppressive narrowness where human conventionality and discipline are in command, where wild drives are exterminated, and where all deviation must be punished. The thought of punishment and supervision, with time, becomes familiar to her; retrospectively, she connects a present feeling of unease with her recollection of transgressed prohibitions and heinous crimes. Quietly, secretly, like a robber in the night, the conscience that belongs to domestic creatures begins to creep into her being. Like a soft current, it steals into her thievish courage, and like an inhibiting fear, it infiltrates her bold strength. Out of the dank twilight there arises slowly something like a disembodied, gray ghost; shadowless it gathers itself into a ball—an uncanny figure which makes one shiver and exposes one.

The wild duck has "ennobled" herself, a word coined by humans; but to herself—that creature born in the wilds of nature—it seems as if she had become sick and sorrowful, helpless and miserable.

And so it can happen one day that people smilingly—and at

the same time mockingly—open a dormer window, without her being able to dare fly out. They know that her prison can be kept open, because stronger than any external bond is the inner one which keeps her in the power of the tamed. So like vain gods, they can take pleasure in the dependency of the captive creature. But they exult too early, because the wild duck eventually does grasp freedom, although it is a freedom different from the one of which she has dreamed. Sitting close to the open window and rubbing longingly against it, she looks upward to the luminous, beckoning heights and then looks shudderingly about her for the specter in the attic room; and then she is seized by a disorienting dizziness. From the depths below, something seems to ascend and grasp slowly after her until she is caught irresistibly, bends ever lower, and plunges down to the courtyard pavement.

In this terrible contradiction and contention between wild and tame, the free and the bound, the world of nature and the world of the attic, there is no solution and no reconciliation:

> *If to the light he finally aspires,*
> *For fear of the nightly ghosts*
> *He would fall with broken wings*
> *From the deceitful windows.*

—*Ibsen*

* * *

Ellida

DESPITE EVERYTHING, perhaps there would be a solution if only the wild duck would not estrange herself from her tame companions and would not stir up a devious revenge against herself in the spirit of the attic world. If only she had been driven into the shelter through need and inexperience, tenderly and modestly, rather than with bold whimsy. She did not know that with her one-time straying from her direct line of flight, she would irrevocably give herself over to captivity. As soon as this is clear to her, she is assailed by a great anguish—wild and powerful—at the loss of her freedom. Restlessly she flutters from one wooden wall to the others, blindly, fearfully straying, beating about with her wings, crouching with somber moodiness in one of the half-dark corners, shuddering frightfully as if at any moment the narrow bounds would come crashing down to bury her in rubble. Hu-

mans and animals futilely attempt to meliorate her homesickness, to offer and grant her everything which could reconcile her
to staying; but she hardly notices any of this and barely notices
that she is being cared for and loved, for despite that she remains
foreign and lonely among them. The image of imprisonment
exclusively dominates her and separates her in her great
abandonment and sorrow from everything that happens around
her. And yet, all her masters and companions do not let themselves feel either injured or deterred, although the wild bird has
affected them with its brooding. The strange charm, the poetry of
nature's wild freedom, which lies over her like magic, awakens
and sustains in their hearts also an empatic inkling of her im-
memorial homeland—a forgotten and distant wonderland—
which she must do without. In fragmentary, enticing pictures,
she conjures up constantly for them that land—while she herself
is tortured by her distorted tendency toward the unreachable, the
unmeasurable, and the horror and fright induced by imprisonment and narrowness. Humans and animals would not idly
watch her incurable dying because of her restless pinings; greater
even than the desire to keep her as their own and to make her part
of the family, grows their love for the poor prisoner. And so they
decided to bid her farewell, as they willingly and sadly open the
window. Then, once again, the wondrous and the inexplicable
occurs—the freed wild duck will not escape.

Further, she does not plunge down into the depths.

It is as if an evil spell of magic drops from her as soon as she is
permitted to freely move her wings. For only her fear of being
captive drove her toward freedom. Her thoughts of flight were
nothing more than a dark fear of chains, the fears of a free-born
creature, which can never be at home in compulsion and slavery.
When love gave freedom back to her, it dissipated the images
created in her delirium; the selflessness of that love-inspired
action proved to her how much for her part she had already
captured her tame companions and how intimately she belonged
to them. Happy and astonished, the wild bird recognizes that it is
she who has conquered the tame world, that she has nested
herself warmly in their love with the victorious magic of freedom
and her wild nature. She recognizes that no longer need she
bashfully avoid what they had for so long and so fruitlessly

offered her, gifts she had failed to notice: protection, communality and friendship. Now she no longer wishes to escape into the boundless, but only wishes that the voluntarily recognized boundaries would no longer be compulsory barriers. She does not wish to misuse her wings, but only let them spread out in free motion, not in order to distance herself from her companions, but to live freely amid their love.

* * *

Hedda

PERHAPS if people can shamefacedly and happily experience such events, they would never again close their attic dormers; they would break apart walls and install large windows so that air and light would surge in unrestrictedly and permit birds to exit and enter at will. With that, the attic room would slowly unfold from a prison into an asylum of freedom, a sanctuary for everything which strays unhoused under the wide sky and which cannot find its way home: a sanctuary for the reconciliation and merging of the tame and the wild. Or it would be comparable with a great, warm nest which lies in sunshine on the roof—as if it were a high watchtower visible and open to all, related to all the countless small wild nests that are created in nature through efficiency and freedom. For there is one place where even the most unquiet urge for wandering and journeying into the distant is calmed, voluntarily limited, and relieved from its striving restlessness—and that is the nest-building springtime of love—a home.

What kind of creature might there be which remains excluded from such a community? It must be a bird who is damned to homelessness among its peers. A bird without a real drive for wandering or journeying into distances because it lacks the courage of those born free in nature, but also because it is full of hatred against protection and peace among companions—she, no less, lacks the sensitivity and gentle disposition of the tame inhabitants. Neither capable of fighting against convention nor of bringing opposite demands into accord, she must forever stew in powerless unrest. She casts no glance into the wide world of freedom outside because, despite all her brightness and beauty, she can only perceive a threatening and empty distance. Yet she is also without perception of the small world around her—even in

the warmest of nests, she sees only confinement. The drive of
both the wild and the tame to create a home is repugnant to her,
and so she lacks the drive for life itself. For that reason there was
for her no possible form of existence in the world of the living
and, above all, the creative; she could not even escape from her
own existence anymore. It may be that falling into other people's
hands relieves life of the superfluous: a quick death in front of the
hunter's gunbarrel.